TRIFLING TO TRIUMPH

Allowing the Gift to Strip my Pride and Save my Life

I0558975

By
Hilton C. Young, Sr
aka Poet GFSoldier

DEDICATION

This book is dedicated to my grandmother, Helen Bennett Johnson. After the death of my mother, Linda Ann Young, who died when I was six, and because of the negligence of my father, my grandmother raised and taught me the value of life, responsibility, and the power of prayer. I thank God so much for a praying grandmother. I know I wouldn't be the person that I am today if it wasn't for her wisdom, guidance, and discipline.

My grandmother had very little education, but her wisdom superseded any degree that a college would give her. She was autodidactic. (Self-taught) With only a sixth-grade education, my grandmother was ahead of her time in entrepreneurship. She ran a very successful transportation business for pre- and elementary school kids. In fact, one of my grandmother's faithful former customers is the mother of, arguably, the hottest hip hop star today. My grandmother transported the customer's son to and from school, and cared for him since he was an infant. Her faith in God is what inspired me to want to go to church and school, and gave me the will to work at being successful. Her love for my sister and me was the kind of love that I have never known anywhere else. I believe with all my heart that her love and prayers were what kept me on the straight and narrow.

She was very hard-working, with an unbelievable work ethic, a very determined woman. She did whatever it took to make sure that my sister and I would have a good life and good education. So the least I can do is try to give back what she has desperately tried to instill in me. Her untimely death is what really made me pick up the pen. I was going through stages of depression and I thought that I would not be able to survive without her. I was so dependent on her for so long that I felt like I was lost without her. So writing poetry is what got me going.

Poetry literally became an escape for me. If I was a mental health patient, then poetry was surely my therapist, writing was my counselor, public speaking was my psychiatrist, and studying and teaching were my prescribed medications. If I needed to vent, the pen and the pad were always there to listen, and with saying that, so was God.

So Maw Maw, this is for you, and thank you so much for inspiring me to do great things. I miss you so much, these last fourteen years have been kind of lonely without you. But God stepped in and took your place when I decided to let go and let Him in. Letting go has not always been the easiest thing to do (still not), but it was for my good to do so. I want to be able to, with God's grace and unmerited favor, live out your legacy if possible, create a legacy for my children, and please God in the process. You were the one who taught me to never give up on my dreams. I hope with all my heart that I am making you a proud woman in heaven as I continue my quest to make these dreams a reality. I will always love you from the bottom of my heart. I hope you're watching me, and I pray that God is with me always.

TABLE OF CONTENTS

INTRODUCTION

From the very start, I was destined to be somebody and not just another human occupying the precious space and time that God so graciously blessed us with. Everyone has a purpose. It may be difficult to see it in the beginning, but it doesn't mean that your destiny is not ever-existing. We have an ever-existing destiny! The question is: When will you start "living" out your ever-existing destiny?

My life was and still is unscripted. However, God's purpose for my life is very much scripted. My life is unscripted because I'm never sure about tomorrow. I only have today. My purpose is scripted as long as I am walking and living in it and not just breathing. Many times, the script that God has mapped out for our lives never comes into fruition because of choices we make, or the lack thereof.

Some of us are choosing to breathe and not live. As long as I am breathing, I have life. As long as I am living, I have purpose. Just because you're breathing, it doesn't necessarily mean that you're living. Just because you have life, it doesn't necessarily mean that you have purpose. You can breathe or exist and still be dead. It only means that you're existing, but not living. While these two words may overlap, it is possible to do one without doing the other. You can't live without existing, but you can exist without living. Chew on that for a minute.

Obviously, we need our existence to live, but we don't need to live to exist. When God breathed into the Adam the "Breath of Life," he became a "living soul," and not just a soul that exists. As long as we are breathing the "Breath of

LIFE," we are living. However, if we are merely breathing air, we only exist. So now we understand that your existence is without question. It's whether or not you're living in your existence that's being called into question.

When animals become an endangered species, it means that their extinction is soon to come, because they're losing their capacity to reproduce or be fruitful. It does not mean that their extinction will come within a few years. Their extinction may come within the next forty years. Just because they are endangered does not mean that they're not producing, but that their numbers are declining at a significant rate. This may suggest that if their productivity may have decreased in considerable measures, it's probably because their ability to multiply may have been lost.

I was born three days **after** my mother slipped into a coma, giving birth to my brother who eventually died. I was a mystery and a miracle child. I was a mystery because no one knew that I was there but God. I was a miracle simply because I was born. To add to that, I was born when my mother came out of the coma, with a badly damaged kidney that was surgically removed six weeks after my birth. Now I will forever live with a scar that reminds me that I am a miracle and that purpose on earth was not an accident.

The concept of this book has been in existence for at least ten years, particularly the title. I always considered myself a **P**erson **O**f **E**motional **T**hought, which is my personal acronym for poet. So whenever I write a poem, I am painting a picture based on the meditation on my own emotions, and then writing it down on paper. Much like an artist who paints on a blank canvas, I would sketch my thoughts. I would begin to talk out my thoughts before I wrote them down or sketched. I would "study" a topic that came to my head and meditate intensely on what I had learned. I would apply the scripture that would best describe the concept I was writing about, and then use the dictionary as my "paint" to bring life or color to the poem that I wrote.

Most poems that I write are written with a sermonic appeal and homiletic twist to it. Poetry is a definite and deliberate effort to preach God's word in a more non-traditional and effective fashion. I've only been writing poetry for about eleven years now, but my ability to speak publicly in front of large crowds has been my gift since I was a child. Poetry is a craft I picked up around the age of twenty-eight, in an effort to get over the death of my grandmother who raised me.

At any rate, this book is now starting to live and does not just exist. As long as the thought to write this book was in my head, it only existed and remained a thought. Now that it is written, published, and you are reading it, it is now living out its true purpose. The thought became alive through this book. Much like God, we are able to speak things He may or may not bring into existence. If scripture lets us know death and life are in the power of the tongue, then it reminds us of how powerful we really are.

So what are you breathing life into? Are you breathing negative or positive things in your life? Are you breathing the right or wrong things over your life? If you're living in one area of your life, then you're dead in the other. If you're living in your misery, you are either dead or existing in other areas. If your depression is alive, then your joy is dead!! So you have to ask yourself: What areas of your life are existing or living? Every day, we go through the living and dying process. Another question to ask yourself is: What's alive or dead in your life? What is alive in your life that should be dead, and is preventing you from living the life that God has for you?

From a figurative standpoint, I breathed life into this book by studying, writing, and publishing it. Just like God breathed into Adam the Breath of Life, we have the power to do the same thing. We are His creation, and we are created in His image, after His likeness. This book will discuss in graved detail some of the events, times, trials, and triumphs of my life and how I overcame and conquered them through the artistic expression of spoken word poetry. My life is, was, and still is a P.O.E.M (Portrait of Emotional Meditation).

I truly believe whatever your purpose in life is, that is what your life is supposed to become. If you are a movie star, then your life will become a movie. If you are a chef, then you express yourself through cooking, and your life can become the best meal you have ever cooked. If you are a preacher, then your life becomes the greatest sermon you have ever ministered. Even if you are a florist or a gardener, we serve the Master Gardner who planted the greatest garden of all time. Your life will eventually become a garden. If you are a hair stylist, make-up artist, architect, teacher, educator, actor, or whatever you chose, are you walking in your purpose? Are you living the life that God has purposed for you?

Eventually your life will become the very thing you are practicing, whether it's right or wrong, positive or negative. Are you practicing the things of God, your own ambitions, or not practicing at all? Are you breathing life into those

4

things that should be dead? For the things of God to manifest themselves in your life, there must be a dying process. The former things that have and still are keeping you bound must die for you to live out God's true purpose.

The poem that follows is my testimony about dead things being kept alive in my life. It's a testimony of how the process of life and death has a continuing process in my life. This poem is carefully based on 2 Corinthians 4:10-12, 16, with the focus on verses 12 and 16. Verse 12 says, "so then death is at work in you while life is still in you." Verse 16 says, "though the outward man may perish and is decaying and wasting away, the inward man is renewed day by day." Think about it this way: For Jesus to have had eternal life, He had to give up His life to get it. Some things have to die for some things to live (2 Corinthians 10-18).

LIFE LIVING INSIDE OF DEATH

My mental strategy

Can sometimes lead to mental tragedy

Not being able to handle the mental capacity

Of my internal struggles with no tenacity

But that's okay because you have not seen the last of me

I apply for jobs but I can't let the fact that I'm black be the reason why you keep passin' me

But if you would just sit down and talk to me then you would see my veracity, my integrity, the significance of my sincerity.

My brain is clogged up with all these thoughts in my mind

Trying to figure out what in the world went wrong with my spiritual designs,

Plots, schemes, devices, plans,

On how I can muster up the audacity, the courage to strengthen my inner man,

I demand,

That the power of God gives me the wisdom to know that I can

Do all things through Christ,

My inner light,

My delight,

Who brought me out of darkness into the marvelous light

Who directs me to walk by faith and not by sight

Who corrects me from all of my wrong doings when I'm not doing right,

Never lets me get ahead of myself, He shares the wealth of my foresight,

Sometimes I can be vindictive and do things out of spite,

But in the midst of His corrections,

I'm going through trials, tribulations, and list of my depressions

At a cost,

I am lost,

Trying to find myself. Was I sold into my own slavery or was I bought,

At a price that I was not even aware of,

That it was His love,

That willingly allowed Him to lay down His life, it's nothing but the Blood.

But my internal struggles can't go unnoticed,

It's something I have to deal with in order to keep my focus

This is not abra cadabra or hocus pocus

I wish I could make my problems disappear with some magic potion.

When I'm hurt I have to deal with the depths of my emotions

Sometimes I feel like everything is moving in slow motion.

So with the pen and the pad I'm lost in a realm of words

Trying to be philosophical on other encouraging things I've heard,

And it becomes distracting

When you began to think that absolutely nothing about you is physically attracting

Being fake and phony by your brilliant acting

Exercising, lifting weights, trying to be cute

Instead of just trying to be you.

Spending way too much time on beautifying the outside

And not enough time on beautifying the inside.

If I am weak inwardly then I must understand and begin to know

That outwardly my weaknesses will begin to show

And know this without a shadow of doubt

That whatever is in you will eventually come out

Because no one will start loving until I start loving myself

I can only be who I am and nobody else.

So as I begin to strategize and prioritize my life I have to realize that sometimes I will be criticized,

By jealousy and envy,

The lack of self-esteem that comes from within me,

Harsh words that come from other people that would offend me,

But why is that?

It is because of my own insecurities

Internal contradictions, conflictions, false intuitions,

and in the midst of my afflictions, unclean impurities,

And it's true to me, not new to me, that

my double-mindedness and ambiguity has to be overcome

by death and spiritual maturity.

It's unforgettable,

There's no way that I can change the inevitable,

I will die some day and I don't even have a schedule,

Of when this particular event will take place

But it's only God's undying grace that keeps me on pace,

To eternal life, not corruption

He never leads me down the road of destruction

Not allowing Satan to come in and kidnap or illegal abduction

God can start adding on to my life or start making deductions

Not falling for whoremonger's smooth words and persuasive seductions

But being obedient to God's word and receiving instructions,

He gives direction,

The strength that is within comes from His internal resurrection

It comes out of my mouth that I believe that I'm saved is confession,

I was made in His image, I am a reflection,

Of the man who created this world in retrospection

Who saved me from the evil tricks of the devil and his deceptions,

That He gave me the gift to spit poetry I have a collection

So basically what I'm saying is the truth about myself,

I have to call upon Jesus to be my help,

There's some things about myself that I have to let go

And really I should've gotten rid of these things from the get go

So as I put this piece inside of a nut shell, I cannot lie

In order for some things to live in me

Some things have got to die.

I know that my body is dying day by day

But my soul and my spirit are being renewed every single day

So if I love my life then I shall lose it

But if I'd be willing to die then Life is what I'm choosing

So my life is what I have to be willing to give.

Because when I live I die, and when I die, I live

So when you see me walking through the valley of the shadow of evil, I will not hold my breath.

Because you're looking at Life living inside of death.

TRIAL TO TRIUMPH

I was always a poor student when I was in school, starting from kindergarten and all through college. I was held back in the first, fifth, and seventh grades. My grade point average never got above a 2.2. I literally hated school. I found school to be very boring and it couldn't keep my attention for longer than five minutes.

When I was in high school, I didn't take college prep courses. All of my high school classes were basic courses except for English, Spanish, and religion. I had to attend summer school to graduate from high school. I was too old to play football my senior year and graduated at the age of twenty. I went through very embarrassing moments while in school. I dealt with extreme bullying and taunting while in grade school for failing three times. I was dealing with the cruelty of being called a dummy, stupid, and retarded. I was also dealing with the fact that there were kids younger than me passing me by, teasing and laughing at me because of it. Kids can be very demeaning at times and very heartless when it comes to someone who may not adjust to school like they do, or do not catch on as fast.

I was one of the kids who could not keep up with the pace of regular classes and needed special education courses to help me throughout my time in elementary and high school. This also took shots at my confidence and my self-esteem. I was also a kid who grew up in the urban city area, but was really shy and timid. What I mean by that was that I was scared to fight. I didn't like confrontation and was afraid to even take up for myself. (I can't believe I'm telling this story. WOW!) I was so afraid at that time while in grade school. I remember when one of my best friends at that time was attacked by a group of boys who went to a middle school around corner from where I went to school. I was so scared that I did nothing to help him. I actually closed the gate so that they wouldn't come after me. Surely I wasn't raised like that, but it still didn't matter. I was too scared to be there for my friend, and it was a hurt that I dealt with for a very long time. It's a hurt that I'm reliving even as I'm typing this, because it's been so long since I have actually talked or written about it.

Dealing with the bullying of being held back for the third time, feeling like a coward, and being called a coward was quite embarrassing and devastating for me. I had suicidal thoughts and I was depressed for a long time. Also, in high school, I tried my best to avoid the taunting from others, so I lied about my age to blend in and be accepted by my peers.

I became very popular because I was a three sport athlete in football, basketball, and track. I became very strong in the weight room. So even the ones who picked on me in grade school thought twice about doing it in high school, because of how muscular I had become. Still, I performed very poorly in the classroom, but that was often times overlooked because of what I did on the football field or basketball court. I wasn't a highly exceptional athlete, however, I was good enough to start at many positions in high school.

At any rate, at the start of my senior year in high school, I ran out of room to lie about my age. I could no longer lie about my age anymore. The truth, in this case, was inevitable. I knew the whole time I was there from the eighth grade to my senior year that eventually I would have to tell the truth about my age. Although my real age was on record with the school and with LAHSAA, I continued to lie to my peers about my age. However, according to the LAHSAA (Louisiana High School Athletic Association) you cannot be nineteen before September 1 of your senior year. Unfortunately, I had a very early birthday and turned nineteen in that February of 1993, before the 93-94 school year, which was my senior year. I was devastated that the time was approaching and I was crushed when I had to come clean. This was a bed that I made for myself and I had to lie in it. Not only did I have to take the responsibility of admitting to my age, but I also had to admit to lying for those five years I was there.

Sometimes we are willing to do anything to avoid being ridiculed and belittled by others. The teasing was not that bad, but it still happened, and it hurt very badly at times, even when I often laughed it off. My teammates joked about it quite often. It hurt, but it was also cool because they tried to make light of the situation. So I graduated at the age of twenty, and when I started college in Iowa I was still behind and had to take remedial courses.

I played football at the college, but had to sit out my first year because the coach didn't think I was good enough. WOW! To be red-shirted at a junior college, I thought I was at the end of my rope. I was thinking that I might as well have quit the team and gone back home. It made me feel as if I wasn't cut out for this. But I stuck with it and practiced all year with the team. I realized that it wasn't that I wasn't good enough, it was the fact that I was an out-of-state player, and there was a limit to how many out-of-state players a team could have. At least, that's what I was told.

At any rate, I initially began to lie about my age again, until I realized that I was in college now and there was no need to keep lying about this, and I stopped altogether. My grades were not poor, but were far from great. I made C's for the most part in remedial courses. Eventually I turned in two good seasons of football at this college and was able to graduate with my associate's degree in psychology. After that, I transferred to a four-year college on a full scholarship with a 2.2GPA. However, I didn't take full advantage of that. My average eventually went down to a 1.8 and my scholarship was in jeopardy. I attended summer school and got my average up to a 1.9, which was needed to eligible to play football by NCAA standards.

I eventually finished my two years of football with a 1.9GPA, which is barely a C average. I didn't graduate from this college for many reasons, which will be discussed later in this book...UNBELEVABLE!! So I moved back home, took two semesters of classes at a local college in my hometown, and then just dropped out altogether. I went through a series of jobs that were neither career- nor goal-oriented occupations, but I did them to keep food on the table and to pay bills.

So I started writing poetry as a way to journal my feelings. It was more like a hobby than a profession. I fathered two babies in 2005...I'll let you figure that one out on your own. Although I continued to do poetry, I had other obligations to attend to.

Also, in 2005 the destruction of New Orleans came about with Hurricane Katrina. At this point, I had to think long and hard about what I wanted to do with my life. I was displaced to Dallas, TX, where I began to take my poetry more seriously. The first event I performed at was a turning point in my life, as poetry took me to another level. I began to minister at churches, open mics, and other venues that would invite me out to perform. Ultimately, poetry prompted me to go back to school in 2009.

I had to start from a status of a junior because not all of my classes transferred. In school, my first class back, I made an A-minus, and it felt good to see a GPA of a 3.67. It felt so good to actually make an A and work hard to get it, that I didn't want to look back. I continued to make A's until I ran into a very hard math class. Eventually, I dropped out again to avoid that class. I stayed out for a year-and-a-half. At that time, I completed my first poetry album. This was the first project or goal I had ever completed. I always started something but never finished it. I experienced some success with the selling of this project. This eventually prompted me to get back into school and finish what I started.

In 2011, I finished my second album and reenrolled in school and finished my degree in psychology in October of 2012, with a 3.7GPA. Now, please understand, I have never made anything above a 2.2. So to accomplish something of this magnitude was a huge turnaround for me.

If it were up to most of the people I've been associated with, I wouldn't be here. I wasn't supposed to be here. But God made a way for me. I realized that my process was pre-ordained by Him, and He is scripting my life in His own way. It's really not my business to know how my life is going to play out. But it is my business to work toward His purpose and allow Him to direct me in this purposeful process. The scripture is very clear when it declares that we should trust in the Lord with all of our hearts and not lean on our own understanding, but all our ways acknowledge Him and He will direct our path. This only acknowledges the fact that He's in control.

There will come a point in your life when things will happen that are out of your control. Worrying won't change it, stress won't deter its inevitability, and doubt will not determine its fate. You just have to give it to God and be done with it. This is the only way that I could've gotten to this stage in my life: giving it to God. I literally had to change.

THE TRANSFORMATION PROCESS
(ROMANS 12:1-2)

There are many instances where we as Christians become masterful in quoting the scripture and often times become champions of memorizing the verses, so much that it almost becomes cliché to mention them. Some have become so skilled in memorizing text that they use their knowledge of the Bible to make it coincide with their own perceptual cognitive thinking capacity. It gets to the point where it becomes redundant to hear the verses, a nuisance to say them, and very aggravating to talk about when there's no substance to elaborate on it.

Allow me to submit to you, the reader, that there may be certain scriptures in the Bible that may be redundant because we have yet to take these scripture to task. Maybe we have become sick and tired of hearing the same thing over and over again because we have not allowed this scripture to be applicable to our everyday living. Please understand: for change to be evident in your life, it must change your entire lifestyle and it is imperative that it starts in your mind.

I remember posting something on Facebook a while ago and it read:

Sometimes we look at the familiarity of scriptures and treat them as if it's cliché to say them. But do we really put these scriptures to task? I've been pondering Romans 12:2 for a while and the thought came to me...if a completed thought comes to my mind, it can only be validated,

18

confirmed, or solidified through my actions. If I never act upon the thought that's in my head, then it only remains... a simple thought, whether it's completed or not. So how can my mind really be renewed if my actions never coincide or intertwine with my so called "renewed" thoughts? (James 2:26) It can only mean that there's either little to no action being exhibited, or my actions contradict my thoughts. My mind can only start the transformation PROCESS, but my actions ultimately determine the transformation PROGRESS. So I guess if I really want to be transformed by the renewing of my mind, then the question is quite obvious....when will I ever walk in it????????

In my opinion, it appears that the scripture is clear in its rendition of everything beginning with a thought. It was thought that ultimately determined the fate of the creation of this earth. It was thought that eventually determined the inevitability of the creation of man. It is by thinking that we create and come up with ideas, concepts, logic, and opinions. It is thinking that makes us who we are. It is what separates us from any other species on the face of the earth. Thinking is what gives us the ability to reason. It gives us the ability to discern or judge correctly or incorrectly. It helps us to develop our intellect. So we have to be careful not to undermine the ability to compose a thought. We must make sure that we remember the significance and the importance of carrying a thought. However, on the other hand, the action actually validates the thought. The word "validate" means to confirm. If there's no action to follow the thought, then it only remains a simple thought.

When God created this world, He spoke it into existence and He didn't stop there. After He spoke it, He also began to craft the things He spoke of. When He said, "Let there be light," it came into existence. However, He had to make light come into action. The scripture says that He made two lights. He made a greater light (sun) to rule the day, and a lesser light (moon) to rule night. Although He thought about it, He also spoke and crafted these things. If the scripture says that faith without works is dead, it reminds me that you can think it and speak it all you want, but until you get up and do the work that you spoke into existence, it will only exist and not live. It only remains a thought.

When God said, "Let us make man in our image and after our likeness," He formed man out of the dust and blew into his nostrils and man became a living soul and not just an existing soul. Every tree bearing fruit after its kind, God created and then made it. Listen family, we have to be able to do more than just think it and speak it. Although these two components are very important, what good is it if we never bring it into action? This is how the transforming process began for me.

For years and years, I was only thinking about the change in my life so much, where it just became lip service whenever I spoke it. Procrastination was one of my biggest downfalls in getting to the next level in my life (Proverbs 1:33). When I started writing, it became an escape for me. Studying what I wrote also became therapeutic for me. It eventually became a guide and an aid for how I expressed myself verbally. It provided me the opportunity to be more in tune with my feelings, and gave me the capacity to explain myself better. I became very good at putting my words together because I found the one thing that actually caught my interest.

So I decided to commit these words to memory and see how other people would respond to them. I began sharing with friends and they would suggest that I go to other events or open mic nights and share my creations. The first response I got when I got behind the mic was overwhelming, and I didn't look back. In 2005, I won my first city-wide grand slam competition against the three-time grand slam champion and future HBO Def Poet, or so I thought. After tallying up the scores correctly, the next day I found out that he actually outscored me by one tenth of a point, and they were only scoring the last poem recited, which received a 30; the highest score one can receive for a poem. Being that they were taking the last poem to score by, it was against the regulations of normal slam rules, which go by the cumulative score, not the individual score. Ultimately, the other guy was declared the winner. We're still good friends today.

However it still felt good to be mentioned in the same company of some of best poets in the city. It was a great accomplishment for me. Nobody knew who I was, and had never heard of a poet named GFSoldier. The fact I came on the scene and impressed people that early was huge! The top five poets made up the New Orleans National Poetry Slam Team, and I was number two. Here I was, an unknown, on the team with two future HBO Def poets, and some of the best poets in the nation. Honestly, I didn't care for second place, but I didn't want to downplay the accomplishment because people were still treating me as if I had won the competition. I went on to compete in Charlotte, North Carolina and Albuquerque, New Mexico that year. It was definitely an honor to experience that kind of competition. It was definitely an accomplishment I will never forget.

THE DARK SIDE OF 2005

Right after the competition, my grandfather got sick and ultimately died a week later. Then Katrina came two weeks after his death. I lost everything in the storm, and two women gave birth to my children, all in that same year. Don't get me wrong: my children are the best thing in my life. It's just that I wanted to do the right thing and act responsibly.

Due to my lack of responsibility, my grandfather dying, and the storm, I fell into a very deep stage of depression. It was actually clinical depression. I was always entertaining suicidal thoughts. I would pray to God and ask Him to take me in my sleep, and then would wake up the next morning pissed because I was living another day in this dreadful prison called earth. I lost all desire to do anything but die. I no longer cared about my hygiene or how I dressed myself. I was fostering the blame for the death of my grandfather, and feeling like I wasn't there for him as much as I should've been.

I was still doing poetry through all of that because it seemed like that was the only thing keeping me alive. Since I didn't care to take counseling, poetry became my only source of therapy. However, in that same breath, none of the poetry that I performed at that time really got to the core of what I was dealing with. So I began to write about what was going on with me at that time. I wrote about my depression, not taking on responsibility for my children (particularly my little girl), and all of the symptoms that go along with depression. I took my pen and released my emotions and feelings onto the pad, committed the words to memory, and ultimately began to recite these issues on stage. Many times in tears, I recited these poems with much pain, passion, and intensity.

This became my catharsis, which is an emotional cleansing of your soul. So this was what ultimately inspired me to go back to school. I went back to school in 2009. When I started school this time around, I worked very hard to see how I would do. To my surprise, I made my first A! It felt so good to make an A, and it felt so gratifying to see that hard work does pay off. That single A was the most impactful occurrence, and it turned my whole attitude around in how I approached school. Making a B was no longer enough for me, and getting a C felt like an F. Ultimately, I graduated with my bachelor's degree in psychology, with a 3.7GPA. I'm now in grad school, studying clinical mental health counseling, with a 3.85 GPA.

MIND RENEWAL

We must begin to have an understanding of what being renewed really means. It is very important that our actions are continually lining up with our constantly renewing minds. I learned early on in grade school that when a word has an "ing" on the end of it, it normally informs us that it's a continuing word, literally meaning the "process of." Whenever something is in process, although it is a continuous action that may come with some interruptions, it is continual without ceasing, or stopping.

Renewing is an unbroken process. I never thought in my wildest dream that I would ever be an A student. This was part of the reason why I was never an A student in the beginning. I always believed and convinced myself that I was a C student. However, God made me in excellence. He didn't make any mistakes. He fearfully and wonderfully made me to the point of perfection, in His image and after His likeness. Why would I consider myself or even settle for being anything less than what God has formed and fashioned for me to be? When you really see yourself as God sees you, you will cease to be inferior.

I was heavily influenced by the people around me. Sometimes I was influenced in good ways, and subconsciously in bad ways. My grandmother influenced me in so many good ways. Although she was Catholic, she was the most praying woman I have ever met. She loved the Lord with all her might, and with all her soul and spirit. Everything my grandmother did to raise me the right way, was always done with the best intentions. However, even when a person means well, it doesn't mean that their methods are necessarily accurate. You can do things with the right intentions and still have the wrong method of doing them. The best intentions do not always bring about the best results. My grandmother was okay with me making C's as long as I was doing my best, as she often said to me. But I *didn't* do my best. I didn't apply myself, nor was I dedicated to making myself better.

Now, don't get me wrong, my grandmother did a godly, excellent job raising me, but it doesn't mean that she did everything right. Parents! Stop telling your kids that they're C students!! Encourage them to do better if they bring C's home. You will begin to see that if you push them to be the best in everything they do, they will excel in every area of their lives. Teach them never to settle for anything less than the very best. And you shouldn't settle for less, either. It doesn't mean that you're bad parents. But as parents you must also strive to become better in every aspect of being a parent. If they need help in certain areas of their academic progress, then you as a parent should not deviate from the responsibility of finding them the right kind of help. But there's absolutely no excuse why they should not make A's. Sorry!

At any rate, in spite of all of the distractions, the setbacks, the ADHD and the extreme procrastination, I was still able to maintain excellence by allowing my thoughts, opinions, perceptions, and logic to change. Dr. Wayne Dyer said it best when he said, "If you change the way you look at things, the things you look at will change." When I went back to school, I found something that sparked my interest. The scripture makes itself clear in Proverbs 23:7, in stating that as a man thinks in his heart, so is he. This is not a figurative statement, in my opinion. I truly believe that you will eventually become whatever or whoever you think you are. Whatever or whoever you think you are, you will eventually take ownership over it. The way you see yourself will ultimately determine your outcome in everything you do, how you live your life, and how others see you.

The process of transformation is crucial and very critical but it is also a very simple process. It is as simple as making a decision and following through with it. It may not be that easy, but it is that simple. We as human beings are such complex organisms, we think at such a rapid pace. We are often over-analytical, and make things more difficult than they really are. However, in contrast to that, we actually serve a very simplistic God. If we learn to master the art of simplicity, we can, more than likely, accomplish more than we set out to do. Why do we complicate what God has made simple? Many times, we doubt ourselves by saying it can't be that simple. As a result, we end up talking ourselves out of doing some of the simple things that success requires. We harbor unnecessary stress because we feel that this is what it takes to get on top. Before long, we end up quitting and give up on our dreams, goals, hopes, aspirations, and ambitions, because at some point we have literally worn ourselves too thin.

This is because, at some point, we have convinced ourselves that life is more complicated than it is simple. We have lied to ourselves and bought into the lie that life is much more difficult than it seems. The truth of the matter is that we have made life more difficult by lying to ourselves. I had to stop lying to myself and make things more simplistic. So I had to start being honest about who I was and who I wished to become.

LYING

This is a very painful section of the book, where I had to deal with one of the most damaging problems that any human being can have. This problem consisted of lying. Lying was probably a daily part of my regimen. I didn't lie habitually, as some do. Well actually I did. But I lied strategically and pathologically. My lies had to have purpose behind them. They had to be lies that had some substance behind them. My lies had to have some firmness to them or some kind of foundation. How oxymoronic is it to say that you have to tell a "substantial lie"? Ponder on that for a minute!

Don't get me wrong. A lie is a lie!! However, when I did lie, it couldn't be a meaningless lie. My lies actually had to mean something. So I had to be observant and carefully perceptive of every lie I told. I actually practiced how to be a good liar. I didn't tell too many senseless lies because there really isn't anything to gain from saying I had grits, eggs, bacon, sausage, and biscuits for breakfast when I only had a bowl of Frosted Flakes. If someone told me that, I would have no reason to think that they were lying to me. It's senseless to say that I wear a size twelve shoe and I only wear an 11-½. However, as I grew older and more knowledgeable of the information I learned throughout studying the Bible and the dictionary, I began to form lies based on things I observed through the scriptures and reading and studying the dictionary. I also carefully observed people and their conversations. I began to talk about things that would happen in the future based on things that were happening in their lives presently. Notice I didn't say prophecy. I would just tell them things that would happen in the future.

Now please don't misconstrue what I'm saying, because every lie will eventually come out in some way, shape, or form, no matter how strategic or well thought out it may be. When I was in high school, I lied about my age to avoid embarrassment and teasing. I also lied about who I was, to be accepted by others. I lied to fit in. I tried to make myself seem better than everybody else. I lied about who I was because I wasn't happy with myself and my life at the time. I wanted to be the A student, the football star, the smart college student, and the all-around famous person. Every single part of my life that I did not like, I lied about it.

Eventually, that had to come to light, because I knew in my senior season I would be too old to play high school football. One thing we need to understand about lying strategically and observantly is that lying can eventually turn into deceptive truth. What I'm trying to say is that when someone is actually telling you the truth, it doesn't necessarily mean that they're being truthful. Telling the truth and being truthful don't always coincide. I say that because if you're telling the truth and your intentions are jacked up, that's worse than any lie you can come up with. Telling the truth with a deceitful heart is worse than lying itself.

I didn't necessarily tell a lie from a verbal perspective, but I had a deceitful heart or a lying spirit. Let's take that conversation between the serpent and Eve for example. In the book of Genesis, chapter 3, there was a discussion between the serpent and Eve about what God commanded of her and Adam concerning the Tree of the Knowledge of

Good and Evil. The question of discussion was, "Did God really say that you shall not eat of 'every' tree in garden?" Eve responded by saying, "We may eat freely of all the trees in the garden. But the tree that is in the middle of the garden we may not eat neither shall we touch it lest we die." This is when the discussion ended and the conversation started. Now, I must be clear in giving the distinction between a discussion and a conversation. Although these two words may overlap, there is a clear distinction between them.

A DISCUSSION VS. CONVERSATION

According to *dictionary.com*, a discussion is an act of consideration or examination by argument, comment, or debate especially to explore solutions. A conversation is an interchanging of thoughts, social intercourse, or intimate acquaintance. WOW! Let's ponder on that phrase for a minute. Social intercourse? Really? I always knew that one can have intercourse physically or sexually. But to have intercourse just by talking or conversing was something that I couldn't fathom when I learned what that meant.

The serpent was literally having intercourse with Eve when he responded by saying, "You shall not surely die," which was still discussion-based and debate-oriented, but what followed was what became very intimate. The serpent went on to say that "God knows that the day that you eat of the fruit, your eyes shall be opened (truth) you shall be like God knowing good and evil (truth)." At this point, the serpent told or verbalized the truth. This particular truth was confirmed when the scripture declared in verses 6 and 7 that when she "saw" that the tree was good for food, and it was pleasing to the sight, and it was desired to make one wise, she took of the fruit and she ate and gave to her husband and he also ate. Then the eyes of both of them became opened. Also in verse 22, God confirmed the serpent's prediction by saying, "Behold man has become one of us knowing good and evil."

When God saw what happened, it was Eve's response that really struck me. Eve responded by saying the serpent beguiled her. To beguile, according to Hebrew customs, means to seduce or trick. She never said that the serpent lied to her, but seduced her. It was the social intercourse that deceived her into thinking that it was okay to eat of the tree. Be careful of people who use the truth to make their lie effective or bring forth their deception. This is what the serpent was best at doing and still is.

When I looked at the etymology of the word serpent, from the Hebrew, it said divine enchanter, which means to attract and "delight" to a high degree. The word delight is an interesting word, because when translating the Garden of Eden it literally means the garden of delight or pleasure. This can only mean that everything in the garden was a pleasure to look at, including the serpent. The serpent looked like it was truthful because of its divine beauty. The serpent sounded like it was truthful because of its intelligent and articulate conversation. The Hebrew also said of the serpent to diligently observe. In that chapter, the serpent listened closely to Eve's response and used her response to its advantage. When Eve mentioned that one should also not touch the tree, that changed or shifted the whole course of the conversation, because God never said not to touch it.

Some scholars believe that by Eve mentioning not to touch the tree, it recognized the strictness of the prohibition. That may be true, but scripture also says in the book of Proverbs that every word of God is pure and He is a shield to them that put their trust in Him. It goes on to say *not to add to the word*, lest God reprove you and you are exposed as a liar (Proverbs 30:5-6).

So then, who really told the first lie? Many people believe that the serpent told the first lie. But here's a question to ponder on: Was the serpent really lying, or being deceptive? I'm only asking because it appears that the one

31

who really told or verbalized the lie was Eve. In the serpent's case, it only appears that deception is at the root of its mindset, and it only piggy-backed on Eve's response. Another point to take into consideration, when it comes to the etymology of the serpent, is that it also means to prognosticate. Prognosticate means to predict or foretell. It's amazing that a snake was able to foretell what would happen to them in the future, but this was a beast that God had made. The serpent predicted that their eyes would be opened and they would become like gods, knowing good and evil.

Where there seems to be a debate is when the serpent said, "You shall not surely die." Question … when the serpent said, "You shall not surely die," was it speaking in reference to eating the tree or touching the tree? When Eve mentioned touching, the serpent could have very well been speaking in reference to not touching the tree, as opposed to not eating it. Have you ever wondered what the serpent's response would've been had Eve never said not to touch it? Hmmm this is an interesting concept. At any rate, Eve not only lied about touching the tree, but she also lied to herself and ultimately was convinced in her own mind that it was okay to eat from the tree. So please understand, when you become good at lying, you are only taking on the spirit of the serpent!!

LYING TO YOURSELF (LYING VS. DECEPTION)

Please understand, before you can lie to anyone, you lie to yourself. That was the big issue with me concerning my lying. I lied to myself and I was convinced that as long as I was telling or verbalizing the truth with my mouth, I didn't have to worry about the deception that was in my heart. I literally used truth to cover up what was really going on inside of me. It was my addiction to deception. I was telling the truth with an untruthful spirit.

Unfortunately, many of us suffer from this addiction subconsciously, and it has become a widespread epidemic. Many people with low self-esteem believe that their confidence will be lifted if they make certain alterations to their bodies, like losing weight, wearing make-up, and exercising, trying to live up to society's expectations of them. Don't get me wrong, all those things are okay. But if you're only doing these things just to boost your deeply rooted self-esteem issues, then you have just lied to yourself.

I lied to myself because I was drawn to the attention that I got from people when I would be deceptive. I was also drawn to the constant flattery and compliments that I got from others, particularly women. At one point, I was abstaining from sexual intercourse physically, but still was addicted to flattery given to me through conversation. My conversation was always good and I always had a way with words. So even though I looked like I was saved and delivered by turning down physical sex, my heart was jacked up! Ultimately, my tongue (conversation) became the penis and the woman's brain (mind) became the vagina.

Much like the serpent, I was very strategic in how I lied. I was very observant in listening to her. I was no longer fornicating physically. I was doing it mentally, emotionally, and socially.

The purpose of this book is to expose how deeply rooted sin can be and how extremely emotions can be drawn or sucked into this. It took me some time to figure out that I was still in sin. Not so much for telling or verbalizing a lie, but using truth to cover up my deception. So I realized that to be truthful, I would have to expose myself in every way possible and rid myself of these serpentine characteristics. I had to expose all my secrets, and all the things I neglected to tell people in all the conversations I engaged myself in.

Normally when one lies habitually, he or she would have to tell more lies to back up the first one being told. In my case, I was good at talking myself out of situations where I knew full well I was wrong, but had the truth to lean on and back me up. My brothers and sisters, please be very careful of those who wrongfully use the truth to defend, justify, and excuse their subtleties or trickery. Man, that was powerful!!! Not only was I exposing myself, but more importantly, exposing the sin that I harbored and housed in my soul.

I strongly encourage you to stop lying to yourself and start living in the truth of who God made you to be. Remember, God is a spirit, and those who worship Him must worship Him in spirit and in truth. So we have to ask ourselves the question: When will we begin to live in the fullness of His truth? When will we stop hiding from the truth? When will we allow the truth to resonate and reside within us, instead of hiding behind the truth to bring forth our own deceptions?

T.R.U.T.H

One of things that I learned about truth is that it has to be exhibited from the inside out, as opposed to outside in. I only say that because if people only hear the truth, but the lifestyle is not applicable to the truth that is told, then we only leave people wondering, "How can this really be truth if the action doesn't coincide?" It reminds me of the discussion between Pilate and Jesus when the Roman governor asked Jesus a rhetorical question, "What is truth? (John 18:38)" I think to a certain degree, this is where Christianity is right now. There too many of us who claim to be Christians who are only *professing* Christ but do not *possess* Christ. The scripture says to confess with our mouths and believe in our hearts. So when Pilate inquired about truth, I believe he asked that question because the same people who sat at Jesus' feet and were healed by His anointed hands were suddenly ready to drive nails through His feet and hands. He was confused just as many non-believers are confused today about truth.

Many people today (non-believers, unsaved, new converts) are asking a very powerful question to the church. If Jesus is who you claim to serve, then why is He not reflected by your daily walk? Why do we persecute people for their sin while arrogantly justifying our sins by clinging to our salvation as if Christians are exempt from reproach? If I wasn't a Christian, I would probably be asking these same questions. It appears that truth has very little meaning or value in the world we live in today because of our lack of drive as Christians to show Christ in His fullness.

I deliberately put the title of this chapter in acronym form for a reason. I think that we as humans don't make truth a reality, but we do make our own perceptions, thoughts, and opinions a reality. I really do believe that a person's perception is their ultimate reality. However, ultimate reality does not mean that it is ultimate truth. So many times, our ultimate reality is not truth. Our ultimate reality is based on what we think is true. Often times, as Paul mentioned to the Romans, we change God's truth into a lie by worshipping the creature more than the creator.

The acronym I came up with is *T*rusting *R*eality *U*ncovered *T*hrough *H*onesty. I came up with that because I believe we use our *perceptions* of truth to cover up what it really is. Much like the Pharisees and religious scholars of biblical times, they used the word of God to justify their twisted ways of thinking. These were people who worshiped God verbally, but denied Him internally. They taught their own customs and traditions, and in turn put God's name on it. The term that comes to mind is sophistry. When looking at the term sophistry, it literally means to take a false statement and make it sound plausible, or to give credibility to something that's not necessarily true.

Many times we give ourselves credibility and use the Bible to validate it. I think it's a very dangerous thing to start using something that's holy to justify unholy things. Many of us have secretly labeled the truth as uncomfortable, irrelevant, not needed, and a host of other things. However, the truth has a way of turning someone's life upside down and inside out. Many times, truth changes us when we really don't want to be changed. There are many things wrong with us that we don't want anybody to tell us about. We have become very comfortable living in our untruths. So as a result, we have made alterations in our lives to cover up the truth that is already in us.

MAKING A CHANGE VS. MAKING ALTERATIONS

Being that we are visual creatures, we often determine who a person is by the things we see and hear. We look at how they carry themselves, how they dress, their conversation, how they talk, the clothes they wear, how pretty the woman is or how handsome the man is. We analyze them from top of their heads to the soles of their feet. We also tend to look at their demeanor, facial appearance, their conduct, mannerisms or behavior, and have a tendency to judge based on those particulars.

The word that comes to mind is physiognomy. This word means to determine the state of a person's character or characteristics from the form or features of the body, especially the face. Another word for this is called anthroposcopy -- anthropo, meaning human, and scope, which means observation.

The truth of the matter is that we really don't know them until we see them in their true element. We know what we see and hear when we see them at church or in a public setting. But do we know who they are behind closed doors? That is the real question. We also see changes in them that we sometime call changes for the better. On the contrary, even though we see a change in how people look, dress, walk, talk, or the car they drive, that does not necessarily constitute a real change. It could really mean that they're only making alterations. Fellas, if you send a suit to the seamstress to get alterations, or the cleaners to be dry cleaned, eventually you'll be picking up the same suit. Ladies, the same goes for you if you ever had a dress altered.

What I'm trying to say is that many people spend years making alterations, yet never step up and make the actual *change*. Don't get me wrong, making alterations is a good thing, but what good can really come of it if you never make the change? I have a friend who I've known for quite a while who, in my opinion, struggled with this. For most of her life she was always plus-sized or full-figured. To let her tell it, she has always been a big girl. Her self-esteem was very low and she was always sad because she could never get the kind of guys she wanted. She would always hear those guys tell her that she had a very pretty face and she was cute, but would not talk to her because she was a big girl. But really the true problem was her confidence.

This was always her story whenever she would talk to me. That she could never get the good-looking, dark-skinned, even-toned small-to-medium-built brothers with muscles and six-pack abs. I always thought she was a very beautiful and attractive woman, but my compliments weren't good enough. She would rather get the compliments from the smaller guys, as she would often express to me. She always wore make-up because she never liked the way she looked without it. The thing was, she always looked good and still does, but she would always say that wearing make-up made her feel better about herself.

She has spent years keeping herself together, which is commendable. She has a very fashionable style. She dresses herself exceptionally well, and when people look at her, they have a hard time figuring out why her self-esteem is low. Many women are intimidated and men are awe-stricken by her astonishing beauty. But she still has insecurities about her body. She eventually got the gastric bypass surgery and lost 135 pounds. Now she was approved for this surgery because of high blood pressure and being pre-diabetic, but that was only used as a cover-up for the real reason why she got the surgery: to be skinny, as she would say. But after losing a very significant amount of weight, she still wasn't satisfied. She also went back into surgery to remove some of the excess skin that came along with a drastic drop in weight. Still, she has insecurities about her body. Now she exercises three to four days a week, which is a good thing. But she's only doing it to win more compliments from the "smaller" "six-pack abs" guys.

It is important to know that you can make as many alterations as you want, but change starts from the inside out, not the outside in. If you're trying to make the change from the outside in, you will forever make alterations and never make the change. This process is only a waste of time. Stop procrastinating and make the change!

PROCRASTINATION

Procrastination has to be one of the most crippling things contributing to the detriment of my progress. I always get the feeling, now that I have arrived, that I should have reached this point sooner, I should have accomplished more, but procrastination got in the way. I have always been a procrastinator. My excuse would be "I'll wait until tomorrow to do it," but tomorrow never comes. Normally, when people put off for tomorrow something they can very well do today, that day usually doesn't come for years or may never come at all.

Proverbs makes a very good point when it says that carelessness kills; complacency is murder (Proverbs 1:32 Mess). It took reaching the age of thirty-eight to finally finish my undergrad degree, sixteen years after my senior season in college. I have a friend who is very gifted in the ministry of preaching and the artistry of singing. However, this person has yet to really explore his gift in a way that would make room for him (Proverbs 18:16). I offered many times to help him out, but there was always an excuse as to why he couldn't do it. Not that these excuses were not legit, but it was the fact that he was leaning and resting on these excuses to justify why he wouldn't.

When God has a purpose for your life, it is the enemy's purpose to distract you. Many times, the enemy distracts us with our trials and tribulations, our shortcomings, imperfections, and inadequacies. Laziness or sloth was one of my biggest setbacks, and why I procrastinated so much. I always felt like I had tomorrow, next week or even next year to do what needed to be done. But those times never came. Dr. Martin Luther King, Jr., said it best when he alluded to accomplishing God's will and purpose over our lives. Our president also alluded to being confronted with the "fierce urgency of now."

I was one who always had to have my eight hours of sleep. But when I started back in school online, I was told in orientation that if you are a procrastinator, being online would either make you or break you. The lady went on to say that this would either help you or hurt you. The reason she mentioned this was because there were daily and weekly deadlines that had to be met. There were research papers, PowerPoint presentations due every week. And of course, there were group projects due every week as well; many of which I facilitated. So I knew that I was going to have to endure a little bit of sleep deprivation if I wanted to achieve great academic success. There were quite a few all-nighters that I had to pull. Then I would go to work that morning without any sleep. Often times I would take a power nap at lunchtime.

However one of the things that online schooling taught me was how to lead, prioritize, and organize, which was something that I was never accustomed to doing. Now, don't get me wrong, I still feel the urge to sleep a lot, be lazy, and put some things off until the next day, but somehow I manage to pull myself together when I feel myself slipping away. The scripture makes this very clear in the book of Proverbs. It says that if you love sleep, your life shall end in poverty, but if you open your eyes and get out of the bed, you will be able to put food on the table and there will be plenty to eat (Proverbs 20:13). Many times, our laziness comes from our stress, especially when we are feeling depressed about something. Normally when we are depressed about something, it saps our strength. However, I could no longer allow that to be an excuse as to why I couldn't achieve all that God intended for me to have.

DEPRESSION

I was very depressed for a long time. I didn't realize how depressed I was until I became comfortable and began to find security in it. I became so insanely peaceful with my depression that I desired to stay in it. I found comfort in my discomfort to the point where I no longer found it uncomfortable. I wasn't happy in my depression because I often acknowledged my extreme sadness. But I became happy with being sad all the time. I know this may sound crazy to some, and in some ways, a bit oxymoronic, but this is an effect that depression can have on some people.

Depression is more than just a psychological condition, it's also a medical condition. Depression will ultimately take a physical toll on the victim as well. To say that one is insanely peaceful in something that can kill them is something to think about closely. God will definitely give us peace in the midst of our storms. I won't deny that. But I don't believe that He ever intends for us to stay there. To be at peace with a situation doesn't mean that your situation is peaceful. I only say that because all hell could be breaking loose in your situation. Trust me when I tell you that it is very dangerous when a person goes into depression mode as way to escape. When depression becomes a soothing place for someone, and they would rather be there than to be somewhere else, it is a definite cause for concern.

One of the symptoms of depression is self-pity, which is probably the most dangerous symptom of them all. More than sadness, lethargy, losing passion or the desire to do the things you once enjoyed, and not taking care of yourself, self-pity will keep you there for an extensive period of time. Many times when I fell into my depression, I felt sorry for myself and often made others feel sorry for me also. It got so bad that some of my friends weren't coming around anymore. It's like I *needed* to feel bad and depressed about something. I became very self-seeking and self-centered in my depression, which is also a symptom. I centered everything around self. It seemed like I always had bad news for people whenever they called or came around.

Eventually I began to understand why people wouldn't call or come around anymore. I will say this: there are some instances where misery loves company. However, in other cases, there are times when, even though you're miserable, you don't feel the need to be around anybody. I experienced both cases. At any rate, you can easily feed that negative energy to somebody else, and they can become drained and depressed just from being around you or talking with you over the phone. I didn't realize that until I actually came out of my own depression.

I have a friend who's also a preacher and at one time, a pastor of two churches. What amazed me about him was that as long as I've known him, he always had something bad going on in his life. He never found the good in anything that was going on in his life. Something was always wrong and he never felt good when I would call to check on him. He always had some kind of drama going on in his life. But I did my best to talk him through it, and still do, because I enjoy doing it. I love to give advice and minister to people when they are going through trials and tribulation because it helps me out and it is very therapeutic to me. Some people can't deal with it and that's understandable, but I'm one of the exceptions to the rule.

Although it grieved me to hear that he was never okay, I was often baffled by the fact that here was a pastor of two churches who counseled, and preached to others about coming out of their storms, and that same word he preached didn't change him. I always wondered: How can the Word effectively help someone of when it doesn't do anything for the person that's doing the helping?

I came to realize that doing certain things such as ministering to someone and giving advice can become more of a task than a passion. His task was giving advice while his passion was depression. Yes, I said it. Sometimes we can become very passionate about the very things that can kill us. That was my issue. Depression ultimately became my passion! Whatever you're giving your time to will inevitably be what you will become passionate about. I know it sounds crazy, but it's very real. Remember, perception is the ultimately reality. Truth is not always connected to reality.

I became physically ill at my lowest point in depression. I suffered symptoms of a stroke in 2007, but the test came back negative. Everything that I complained to the doctor about was all symptoms, but the test showed something different. Two years later, I suffered very badly the symptoms of strep throat. However, that test also came back negative. Although the tests were negative, I still had to take the medication to treat the symptoms. Then I began to understand that depression and anxiety are medical conditions as well as psychological conditions.

Due to the fact that I was suffering these medical conditions, it prompted me to start writing down my issues as a way to deal with them, and eventually my journaling turned into poetry. I really began to minister to myself and listened to my own advice.

MINISTERING TO OTHERS

Many times we give good advice, but we very seldom listen to it or receive it. Many times we tell people what to do, but don't allow other people to tell us what or how to do things. Of course, that's a whole different topic altogether that will be addressed later on in this book.

Now, I want to preface something by saying this: When you're giving someone advice, especially while they're depressed, you have to be very effective and sensitive to the person who's going through a trial. The scripture says to be wise as the serpent but harmless as a dove (Matthew 10:16). It also says that a soft answer turns away wrath or anger (Proverbs 15:1). In the book of James, it says that we should be slow speak and quick to listen (James 1:19).

Often times, we are the exact opposite of what the scriptures tell us. Many times we are quick to speak when the person needs more of a listening or discerning ear. We should really devote our time to being ready and attentive listeners. If we can be more understanding with our gestures than our mouths. It can prove to be much more effective. Sometimes a person needs a head nod of empathy, which can be one of most powerful forms of endearment to someone who's going through difficult times.

Sometimes the best technique in ministering to someone doesn't require us to speak at all. If you're doing most of the talking, then you make the whole conversation about you, whether you think you're giving good advice or not. When you're attentively listening to others, you make it about them. When a person is in emotional distress, it is comforting to know that you have their best interest at heart. When you are intelligently hearing someone, which is the definition for discernment according to Strong's, you will know whether or not to speak. Another powerful definition that comes to mind in reference to discernment comes from the book *Intentional Interviewing and Counseling,* is to listen with intention, with love, and with the "ear of heart." Listen not only cerebrally with intellect, but with the wholeness of feelings, our emotions, imaginations and ourselves (Ivey, Ivey, & Zalaquett, 2014).

You will ultimately know when it's the right time to give advice or not. You will inevitably know when to give advice or feedback, even when they don't verbally ask you for it. I've grown very skeptical of the word "advice," so I would rather say feedback. Feedback doesn't always require a verbal output. Many times, people's gestures or mannerisms will tell you they are longing for good, sound feedback. Also, when listening attentively and hearing intelligently, we should listen with an empathetic ear, which means that you're hearing with a sensitive ear while simultaneously listening with a critical ear. Yes, you intuitively understand what they are feeling and are able to imagine the world from their perspective. But it does not mean that you will necessarily agree with them. You will not condone all of their actions or decision making, but you will understand why they have taken such an action or made such a decision.

I believe that although these terms are similar and synonymous, hearing and listening have a very distinctive difference. Hearing is something that most humans are naturally born to do. However, listening is an acquired skill. To possess the skill of listening is developed over a period of time. So if we want the feedback we give to be welcomed, we must learn how to constructively criticize them. So, when we do give concrete or constructive feedback, it can be often the best information that has ever been given.

I think the real reason why we don't listen to our own advice is because we forget about it when it is given, or we don't think it applies to us. I believe wholeheartedly that any good advice we give will always apply to us first. I've come to realize that when I reach deep inside myself and pull out some concrete advice, it's like having a conversation with God and letting the person I'm ministering to in on the conversation. So in a real sense, God is counseling me and I am merely telling the other person what was told to me.

I want to submit to the reader that when God is talking to you, more than likely it is for the purpose to help you first and then the people you minister to. There's liberty in knowing your advice has helped you and delivered you from a troubled or shameful situation. However, it is tragic when the information or advice you give doesn't have any effect over your own life circumstance. It is catastrophic when your advice applies to everyone except the reflection you see in the mirror.

Now on the other hand, there are many times that we listen to our own perceptions and we put God in them. Not that we're not telling the truth, but now the truth is being used in a non-constructive way.

DESTRUCTIVE CRITICISM VS.
CONSTRUCTIVE CRITICISM

Many times we have good intentions behind the advice we give, and a good heart when we criticize people. Sometimes we're giving the truth. But very often, we are giving our *versions* of the truth, or our "opinionated truths." We have very imaginative and colorful perceptions of how we see things, and when we criticize we sometimes believe that everyone should see the world the way we see it. With that thought in mind, we sometimes tend to treat people in a very condescending manner when they don't see things exactly how we see them. As a result, when we give critical advice, we tend to give good information in a very condescending tone or manner.

Whenever something is under construction, it is in the building process. It only means the architecture is not yet complete but it is being built. So think of giving advice as a means of being under construction. So, now then, when you're giving constructive criticism, the information is used to build someone up and not tear them down. If you're always focused on the negative aspect of what someone does, and never acknowledge anything positive or good characteristics of what they do, then you are only using these truths to tear that person down. When you build someone up, you focus on their strengths and how they can better themselves using the strengths that they already have.

That was one of the things that helped me along the way. As I mentioned earlier in this book, it was my ability to speak and write that ultimately motivated me to go back to school and approach school from another perspective. My strengths, gifts and talents gave me the push to excel at my fullest potential. I graduated with a 3.7GPA, and I still haven't reached my greatest potential. Now, having the capacity to further my education gives me the opportunity to reach certain heights I would never have known existed if I hadn't explored my strengths. If you can tell people how they can possibly better themselves without tearing them down, then you can successfully build them up. If you're only tearing them down, which means to criticize them on every little wrong they have done in their lives, then you're not helping matters. If you never acknowledge anything they do that's good, and only wait until they do something wrong to open your mouth, then you're only making the person feel as if they do everything wrong.

This is called destructive criticism. Consider that whenever something is under destruction, then it is normally ready to be destroyed or torn down. When a building is being considered or scheduled for demolition, it is ready to be torn down. If your only purpose in life is to open your mouth whenever you see wrong occur in someone, then you're only participating in the mental destruction of the person you're intending to help. Furthermore, when we do things of this magnitude, it is often because we see a deeper sense of ourselves in that person, and in turn criticize them to prevent others from seeing those same characteristics being exhibited in our own lives.

So in a deeper sense, we can't really help that person or find a solution for them because we have not found a way to rid ourselves of that negative thing. So we continue to falsely build ourselves up with a corrupt thinking capacity, validating ourselves, self-certified to tear people down by distortedly convincing ourselves that there is some good that can come out of it.

I have a very good friend who's also a preacher, who carries and conducts herself in the fear of the Lord. She really loves the Lord and is very dedicated to what she does as a minister. She is very proficient in giving sound advice, giving correction where needed, and rebuking when necessary. Unfortunately, however, she can be very deficient in how she gives the advice, correction, criticism, or rebuke. Particularly, she can be extremely deficient in how she receives correction, criticism, and rebuke. There are times when she gives criticism in an extremely destructive and condescending voice tone. When she's often told about it, she immediately tries to justify what she does with scripture.

One of the most damaging things that one can do to themselves is belittle someone, then put a God label on it to validate and justify it because it was truth being said. Just because there was truth to what you said, that doesn't necessarily mean God laid it upon your heart to say it. This is especially true if the advice was given in a condescending manner. We cannot justify everything we do with the truth, especially when it doesn't apply to us. In essence, it is more or less a pre-conceived notion of the truth that often leads us down the path of destruction when giving advice. My friend really thought that she was helping someone, but only ended up hurting the person. Be careful of what you do with the truth, because it could hurt and tear down when it should be used to build someone up.

MISHANDLING THE TRUTH

With that being said, my good friend would always respond by saying, "They can't handle the truth." Okay, well, let's examine this for a minute. I came to realize that when somebody has the unmitigated audacity to say that someone can't handle the truth, it is often because the person giving it can't handle the truth themselves. The scripture is clear when it says that one should be wise as a serpent, but harmless as a dove. It also says that a soft answer turns away wrath.

Normally, attention is hardly ever given to the person who's giving the truth, but rather the attention is given to the recipient of the truth, regardless of how it is given. If the truth is given harshly and not harmlessly, then the person giving the truth is guilty of mishandling it. Normally when truth is being mishandled, more than likely the person receiving won't be able to handle it either. I think I have to say this again. Normally when a person cannot handle the truth, it is because the person giving the truth cannot handle it correctly either.

Consider this: If someone were to eat a well-cooked porterhouse steak at one of the finest steakhouses in your town, in most cases, they would have to use a fork and a steak knife to assist them in eating it. For them to be able to digest the steak properly, they would have to cut the steak into pieces and eat the steak one piece at a time. The next step is to chew the piece of steak at least fifteen to twenty times to make it soft enough, or until the steak is sufficiently pulped to allow you to swallow. And often we will have a drink of our favorite beverage to help wash it down. Then that same process starts all over again with the next piece. 1. Cut. 2. Eat one piece at a time 3. Chew each piece fifteen to twenty times. 4. Swallow. 5. Drink.

It is said that it takes the body twenty-four to seventy-two hours to completely digest red meat. Also, if partially cooked meat is swallowed, it can bring stress to the digestive system. Another fact that's important to note is if too much is taken in at a time, or we eat too fast, it can cause heartburn and indigestion, which can cause the body to regurgitate its food. I'm going somewhere with this.

OBJECTIVE TRUTH VS. SUBJECTIVE TRUTH

When truth is objective, more than likely it can be accepted because it's not directly focused on one thing or person. That kind of truth can be considered or taken as a donut, a slice of your favorite cake or pie, or a scoop of your favorite ice cream. However, when truth becomes subjective, it may not be easily accepted, especially when subjective truth focuses more on the individual than the object. Also, when this truth is more corrective than it is commending as it relates to the individual or the subject, it may come off as offensive to some.

The point I'm trying to make is that we should consider the subjective truth as a steak. We should strive to make the truth as easy to swallow as possible, especially when we're dealing with babes in Christ. We should consider chopping or cutting the truth into small pieces, and feed this to the people we minister to, one small piece at a time. When dealing with babes in Christ, that piece should be even smaller, especially when you're trying to wean them off of milk. If the scripture says that we should rightly or properly divide the word of truth, then we should probably gain some wisdom first before we speak in those regards. No one -- and I do mean no one -- can handle the truth being shoved down their throats, regardless of how mature a person thinks he or she is. We would all regurgitate if God were to give us the truth in that capacity. If we continue to mishandle the truth for the sake of wanting to be right all of the time, then you should surely expect the person you're giving it to not to handle it very well.

KILLING THE OBSESSION TO BE RIGHT (I TOLD YOU SO)

I was one who always had to be right in everything that I said or did. I just couldn't be wrong. Even though I have been wrong many times, I would find a way to be right. Now, I know I'm not talking to none of y'all. But this is one of those things that I still struggle with from time to time. Many times this struggle came about because of pride, stubbornness and extreme egotism. I just had to be right at whatever cost, even at the expense of losing a soul. I always walked away with my head held up high because I did win the argument -- but I lost souls. I had to win.

Allow me to submit to you that being right doesn't necessarily mean that you are right.

Let me go deeper. Just because you are correct with your facts does not always mean the timing was right for you say it. Many times, we can have the wrong intentions when we're trying to be right.

So as a result, you can be correct and still be wrong because you lack the wisdom to be able to exercise sound judgment in your decision to speak in an orderly manner. Yes! Sometimes you can be right at the wrong time. Which means you were correct in the information you provided, but you rudely spilled the information out due to lack of sound discipline. You were ethically right and morally wrong. Therefore, as a Christian there has to be a balance of morals and ethics, and one should not exceed the other. If a person is being resistant and not receptive to what is being said, and you feel the need to spill it out anyway, then you're only being a self-indulgent fool who's more concerned with being right than showing concern for others. How selfish is that?

This is for people who feel the need to have an "I told you so" moment. Saying "I told you so" doesn't help anyone!! It only further boosts the ego of the person who says it. To exercise good judgment, you have to give up your right to be right. You have to be able to get rid of all your "I told you so" moments. I have lost good friends from trying to be right. I realized that I had to change or I would run everyone away from me.

I have a friend who still, to this day, has to be right about everything. She has literally run everyone who has cared about her away from her. Her excuse is that these people could not handle her realness. I used to say the same thing and realized it was really stupid. You mean to tell me that this is the excuse for *everybody* who has walked away from you? I want to be truthful with you, the reader. If you have already given someone advice and they have done what is contrary to advice given them, they're probably beating themselves up for it. They don't need you throwing it in their faces. More than likely, they have acknowledged that you were right, whether they verbalize or not. So why do you feel the need to pat yourself on the back with an "I told you so" moment?

People who are obsessed with being right often times don't know or acknowledge that they're actually being that way. There's nothing more dangerous than a self-righteous, stubborn, self-indulgent fool who's right all the time and never wrong. It normally means that they're not open to anyone's opinion but their own. Even if you have proven them wrong without a shadow of a doubt, they'll find a way to be right. If I had to diagnose these people, I would say that they are narcissistic. At any rate, I used to be this way and I used scripture to justify everything I did and said. Not that I would study the scripture in full context, but I would memorize certain verses and became good at quoting them. I became a fool who was wise in my own conceit.

STUDYING SCRIPTURE VS. QUOTING
BIBLE VERSES

There's big difference between quoting Bible verses and actually studying the scripture. There are those who become champions in quoting Bible verses. As a result, they become sore losers in studying the text. When you exemplify poor ability to soundly and intelligently present the text, quoting Bible verses becomes nothing more than mere gibberish conversation. Consider the text.

2 Timothy 2:14-16

Amplified Bible (AMP)

[14] Remind [the people] of these facts and [solemnly] charge them in the presence of the Lord to avoid petty controversy over words, which does no good but upsets and undermines the faith of the hearers. [15] Study and be eager and do your utmost to present yourself to God approved (tested by trial), a workman who has no cause to be ashamed, correctly analyzing and accurately dividing [rightly handling and skillfully teaching] the Word of Truth. [16] But avoid all empty (vain, useless, idle) talk, for it will lead people into more and more ungodliness.

The Apostle Paul emphasizes to Timothy the importance of studying the scripture. The Amplified version of the Bible stresses the importance of rightly handling and skillfully teaching the Word of Truth. This scripture really brings light to how we can sometimes mishandle the truth. So I want to be very deliberate in saying this again: if you are mishandling the truth, then do not expect the person on the receiving end to handle it well.

The scripture also says that discernment is found on the lips of him who is skilled in godly wisdom. However, the rod of discipline is for him who lacks sense and understanding. It goes on to say the wise man stores up his knowledge, but the mouth of the foolish is a present destruction (Proverbs 10:13-14). In my own mind, I had all the answers and no one could tell me differently. I became a fool who had knowledge, with no skill or ability to properly use or speak that knowledge.

The scripture tells us that there is more hope for a fool than for the one who is wise in his own conceit (Proverbs 26:12). And if you see him, don't waste your breath on trying to speak any wisdom to this fool, for he will despise the wisdom of your words (Proverbs 23:9). Although you may have the wisest advice for him, it wouldn't be good enough to reach him, especially if he or she has the "know it all" attitude. I wrote a poem about this particular thing because I had to get delivered from this form of pride. It started not to feel good to be this way, and so God rebuked me harshly with this one. So I had to share this with you:

STOP SMELLING YOURSELF

God has given you a gift and has blessed you with favor

But your arrogance has swallowed you whole because of the olive green color on your paper.

You think you're all of that because you have a title?

You think you're holier than thou because you can articulate the holy Bible

You're so full of yourself that I don't think you get the picture

That you are supposed to humble yourself because Satan himself knows the scripture

Because of your position you think you're better than everybody else

But when you think that you're something when you're nothing you deceive your own self

It's obvious you need to evaluate yourself because apparently

You don't know that to fear the Lord is to hate evil, pride, and arrogancy

Don't you know that you're headed for your own defeat?

Because there's more hope for a fool than a man that is wise in his own conceit

I know that God has blessed you with a gift and I won't doubt it

But when you know who you are in God and the more mature you become

It's the less you have to brag about it!

You think you're all of that because you pastor 40,000 people

And now you think that these people are beneath you instead of your equal

God has graced you with the gift to exegete the text and preach to me

But you're so stuck on yourself that after service you don't even speak to me

Because you're preaching to people who have dreams, goals and aspirations

And if your desire is to teach us then you shall receive a greater condemnation

You are supposed to be a living example of what a true person is supposed to be

You're job is to feed and shepherd the flock because that's what you chose to be

You are supposed to give us a better insight on how we are to serve the Master

And I don't care if you're teacher, preacher, prophet, doctor, poet, bishop, evangelist, minister, reverend, elder, singer, deacon, usher, or a pastor

I don't need a seminary scholar student and theological geniuses

With your fake hallelujahs and your phony "thank you, Jesuses"

Because I don't care what you learned in the seminary or in college

Because you're arrogant then my people shall be destroyed for a lack of knowledge

You egoistical stuck up conceited individual

Your attitude is stank ugly and despicable

You like to hear your own self talk and it's pitiful

And you're not supposed to be carnally minded but spiritual

You see you're just like the fool who loves to utter all of his mind

But your attitude is supposed to be one that is gentle and kind

You can rebuke if you have to. Go right ahead, I don't mind

Just make sure that your spiritual walk with the Lord is in line

Because open rebuke is better than secret love

But I would rather have God to chastise me than for other hypocrites to judge

Because my Lord and Savior Jesus Christ is the One who really paid the way

And if you cannot submit yourselves to God, then what shall we say?

Shall we continue in sin because we're no long under law? God forbid!

Because you really didn't make self that anointed and powerful, God did

And I hope to God I'm not reciting to a bunch of fools

Because I believe in the scientific gravitational rule

That what goes up must eventually come down

And your gift has elevated to the sky but your character has brought you back to the ground

And I know that sometimes you will fall short because we all do

But don't preach to me and act like the scripture does not apply to you

Because you know that you yourself have done some of the same things that we do

So humble yourself like the crooked tax collector in the book of Luke

And some of y'all may not like some of things that I'm talking about

But the truth is if you can't say amen, then you can always say ouch

Because I had to grab a mirror and talk a long look at myself

And take responsibility for my problems and no one else

Because success is not only based on money, fortune, fame and wealth

So please take heed to this as I boldly and humbly say STOP SMELLING YOURSELF!!!

EXAMINE YOURSELF

"Stop smelling yourself" was an old phrase my grandmother effectively used to get me in order whenever I spoke too highly of myself, especially when I thought I was superior over everyone else. Whenever my grandmother would catch me acting in such a way, she would tell me in a very strong, authoritative voice and southern country "Louziana" accent, "Boy, ya smellin' yaself." LOL!!! Immediately I knew what that meant. Although my grandmother had only a sixth-grade education, her wisdom was unparalleled and insurmountable. My grandmother was not a student of the Bible either, but the wisdom she spoke was scripturally based and Bible-oriented. Paul eloquently defends my grandmother's old phrase with his declaration to the Roman church:

Romans 12:3

Amplified Bible (AMP)

[3] For by the grace (unmerited favor of God) given to me I warn everyone among you not to estimate and think of himself more highly than he ought [not to have an exaggerated opinion of his own importance], but to rate his ability with sober judgment, each according to the degree of faith apportioned by God to him.

So we must be able to look deep within ourselves and examine our motives, intentions, and thought processes behind everything that we do. We have to be careful to evaluate ourselves daily as it relates to the information we're using for the glory of God and not the glory of men.

"Stop Smelling Yourself" was written in reference to people who have taken God's gift and have glorified themselves with it. The examining process should be an ongoing and never-ending process of a daily evaluation of ourselves, with the emphasis on growth and maturity.

When you consider yourself a person of wisdom, you're never closed-minded to the maturation process. Once I developed that process, I was less eager to prove someone else wrong. I was less likely to boast about how right I was. I began to clearly see and understand how wrong I was. I realized that as I examined my wrongdoings and become transparent in expressing them, learning, and teaching deliverance from them, then I would be less likely to receive harsh punishment and rebuke from God. Also, people would be more receptive to what I had to say and in turn be convicted by my own testimony.

1 Corinthians 11:31-32

Amplified Bible (AMP)

31 For if we searchingly examined ourselves [detecting our shortcomings and recognizing our own condition], we should not be judged and penalty decreed [by the divine judgment].

32 But when we [fall short and] are judged by the Lord, we are disciplined and chastened, so that we may not [finally] be condemned [to eternal punishment along] with the world.

Whenever we begin to truly examine ourselves, this is where integrity meets character. This is the conduct that is required of the person who claims to be Christian, which means to be Christ-like. For us to build our character, we must first become transparent about who we are and be honest with ourselves. I truly believe that honesty is the foundation for growing to the level of integrity, especially when it comes to self-evaluation and examining ourselves. But I must stress that we should not just rest on mere honesty.

Honesty vs. Integrity

I know this may seem perplexing in a sense, because these two words are similar and they can very well overlap. It was even difficult for me to make a clear distinction between these words. So let me start with brief definition of them.

Honesty, according to *dictionary.com*, means the quality of being honest; uprightness and fairness. It goes on to say truthfulness, sincerity, or frankness; freedom from deceit or fraud. Integrity, on the other hand, means adherence to moral and ethical principles or soundness of moral character.

However, life's experiences are probably the best teacher, at least in my case. When looking at the dictionary's meaning of both words, there appears to be a clear distinction, in my opinion. You can be a very honest person, but it doesn't necessarily mean that you have integrity. For example, if a person admits to being a liar, thief, drug dealer or serial killer, and he continues to steal and sell drugs, admittedly he's being honest about what he does. He admits to his wrongdoing, but continues to do it. This tells me that while he is honest, he lacks moral character or integrity. He's being truthful about who he is and the wrong that he's done, but he admits that he won't stop until he gets caught. While honesty tells me that he's being truthful, integrity tells me that this is wrong. Although I can benefit from this action financially or monetarily, there will be harsh consequences to suffer and stiff penalties that will be handed down if I follow through with it. Integrity is doing the right thing in spite of the benefits of wrongdoing.

It appears that honesty is doing what's right in the presence of people, while integrity is doing what's right in the absence of people. This was my story. I thought that if I was only honest about who I was as a person, then that was enough. I didn't know how important integrity was. I thought that as long as I was truthful, up front, and frank about who I was, that would be the most sincere thing I could do. But I soon found out that sometimes one can be sincere and still be wrong. I was sincerely wrong in many of my ways. Sincerity does not always exude integrity. Although I had sincere reasons for doing some of things I did, such as lying, cheating, and other mischievous things, it still didn't make it right.

I was a coward! I refused to do the right thing because of the fear of what people would think of me. So I made people believe I was something or someone I wasn't. I was not a big fan of me. I did not love myself. So I said things about myself that were not true. I was afraid of being me because I didn't want to be teased anymore, and didn't want to be a laughingstock of the group.

However, I eventually discovered that whatever goes on in the dark will ultimately come to the light. I always thought this statement was just cliché until it happened to me. I realized that I was only doing more harm than good to myself. Although it may have appeared to be real, I realized that my actions were not lining up with my words, and soon others were beginning to realize it too. I realized that integrity was not only doing the right in public, but also doing the right thing in private. My grandmother always did the right thing, no matter the consequence. I learned a lot from my grandmother, but obviously did not apply it.

So I must submit to you, the reader, that integrity is truly exhibited when no one is looking. It wasn't until late in my life that I realized that being the best me I can be was the most rewarding thing I could've ever done. I discovered that while the admission of one's flaws is an act of honesty, it is only a fraction of what integrity is. This is what makes the separation between what's moral and ethical, because what's ethically right can be morally wrong. My good people, don't wait years and years to become a person of integrity, like I did. Please don't waste precious time and years away, trying to be someone you're not. Don't prostitute yourselves for the sake of trying to get people to like you, and lose yourself in the process

PROSTITUTING THE GIFT

This topic is the quintessential example of where to draw the fine line between what's moral and ethical. This is also a very difficult thing to talk about, because there are not too many artist/poets in the body of Christ who are willing to admit to this particular charge. Many times, this particular thing is hard to detect when the poet/artist is in ministry mode. At any rate, this was a big issue with me. I was so into giving that stellar performance that many times I blocked out my assignment to minister to the people of God. The applause, the finger snaps, the high fives, the compliments, and loud cheers were mostly my concern. I did not care about winning souls more than I cared about my pride, my ego, and popularity.

I was diligently ethical in ministering God's word through poetry. But morally I was wrong, because my heart was in the wrong place. Now, this doesn't apply to none of y'all other artists and poets because you have never done such a thing. However, I can't lie about this thing. I have to die to myself daily, because sometimes it is still a struggle. Y'all don't want to hear me talk about this thing!! I think if we as artists are honest with ourselves, we can all admit at some point in our ministries we have been flattered by the attention that comes along with having a good ministry that others are drawn to, because of the anointing that God has on the recipient of the gift. Maybe that's not the case for some, but that's the case for me. It was and still is very flattering to get this kind of attention. I was more worried about getting my shine on than I was about helping people, because I was getting the kind of attention that I never had before. If didn't get a standing ovation every time I touched a mic, I would be mad or upset. Although I was impacting at the time, it didn't matter because I was more concerned about the attention than I was the asceticism. I was more concerned about me getting seen by others than self-denial. I would exemplify false humility.

False humility is sometimes hard to detect when one does not look beneath the surface. Often times, we scratch the surface, having never taken the time to go beneath it. I was saying "thank you" to the compliments, but I realized that even when saying "thank you," I was still taking the credit for what God had and still is manifesting. So I began to say "Praise God" to every compliment I would get, making sure that I would acknowledge God every single time.

Parenthetically, I must admit that when something is deeply rooted in you, it will take a lot more than "Praise God" and "To God be the glory" to get rid of it. Yeah, that's right! I was saying "Praise God" and still being lifted up in pride. However, when the attention, the accolades, and all of the superficial and monetary gain that come with having the gift become the only things the artist/poet desires, then it is no longer about ministry, it is just a performance, and the only objective is to entertain. Whenever your ministry becomes subjective, then you become your own focus. When the focus is more on the individual and less on the God who's instrumental in speaking through the individual, then the people only see the individual, not God.

Sadly, the tragedy comes when the people leave, having only been entertained and not ministered to. So some of them exit the same way they came in. There will be some who will actually get some substance out of what's being performed, but God will definitely not be pleased with this.

71

So in essence, my ethics were in right standing but my morals were fraudulent. My morals were fraudulent because my motives and intentions were jacked up. So as a result, I began to take a very steep plunge into the spiritual realm of prostitution. I began to sell my soul for outward praise, but inwardly I was falling out of relationship with God. I was ministering and backsliding simultaneously. I know this may sound strange and hard to grasp, especially when you are touching lives in the midst of backsliding. How can one perform, minister, and backslide at the same time? For me, although I was performing, and that performance ministered to the people, I was more concerned with their applause, the self-glorification, rather than the glorification of God. That alone is how one can backslide and minister at the same.

Allow me to submit to you, brothers and sisters who desire to be in the position to speak to the masses through spoken word poetry, or any area of verbal and non-verbal artistry. Just because Jesus is coming out of your mouth doesn't necessarily mean that He's on your heart. Just because you speak about God doesn't mean that God is on your heart. This is the most important thing that I had to come to grips with. I had to allow God to uproot the things that were not like Him. I had to come into the understanding that I was not being true to myself, let alone to God. I was saying, "Praise God," and still taking the credit. I was still saying, "Jesus," and trying to impress people.

I'm not going to lie about this, because this is an everyday struggle. It actually got to the point where I became depressed if the crowd did not react in the way that I expected them to. I felt if I got a poor applause or response, then I must've given a poor performance. Even though I would still have people come up to me and bless me for blessing them, it was not enough. I had to have everybody on their feet, or it was not successful. Now that I'm looking back on it as I'm typing away, it's beginning to make me sick just to think about how trifling I was in that regard. I lost my focus and began to give my attention to the masses instead of the one. I ignored the one who came up to me and told how much I helped them, because everybody didn't applaud. Please hear me, my brothers, sisters, fellow artists, poets, and ministers: If your focus becomes anything other than what God wants it to be when you are operating in your gift, then you have just subjected yourself to a backslidden stage of your ministry.

If God is no longer the object or the subject in which you minister to the people, then you are literally destroying yourself from the inside out and you have prostituted yourself for the sake of outward attention, while neglecting yourself inwardly. As I said before, this is a continuous fight to stay humble and not be hung up on pride. The only way that you can ever be delivered from something is by total self-admission and God-submission. If there's no admission, there can be no remission. This is where integrity plays its part.

I believe that integrity is what's missing in today's society. We paint the picture of illusion instead of painting the picture of resolution. Illusion is only good for the moment. The question for me is: How can you truly have an impact if what you write and recite is only good for the moment? How can we resolve anything if there's only instant gratification, short-term pacification, and not long-term edification? This is my story. This is what I write about. This is why I put myself out there in open shame or public humiliation. I do this to be a living example of how arrogance was not who God wanted me to be, but what I allowed myself to become. And sometimes I still struggle to stay delivered. I must keep real. It's the only way I know. Yes! I still struggle with pride!

Please understand this. Once you have fought to get delivered, you will have to fight ten times as hard to stay that way. Don't ever think for a second that you have finally arrived, just because God has delivered you from something. Because the temptation begins to intensify abundantly once you are delivered. You must be able to walk in your deliverance every single day of your life without taking any days off. And the reality of this is that sometimes I took some days off. You will sometimes take days off as well, simply because you are not perfect. But the main thing is consistency. If you have no consistency, you are no better than the crack addict that's fresh out of rehab and going back to the crack house. This poem is a warning for every artist, poet, motivational speaker, musician, author, or any gift in the area of artistic expression. You really need to get your pride in check!

PRIDE CHECK

Why are you here?

Are you truly ministering to edify the hearts,

Minds, and souls of people who have ears to hear?

Or are you doing this for all of the applause, the honor, the accolades, the standing ovations, the compliments, and the loud cheers?

Trying to gain the approval of your peers

But the question is: Is it God?

Or is it the people that you fear?

See, I used to think that power of God's anointing on my life

was predicated upon how many people can fill up the seats

Not realizing that power of God's anointing is actually predicated on

how many souls can be reached.

It was almost like it was a competition and I was more worried about putting on a good show and how many artists I can beat

But my contemptible worthless victory was detestably minute

and vaguely obsolete

And then I ultimately came to the conclusion that actually

Satan's victory and my defeat.

You so busy trying to impress other people with you are a charismatic orator.

But if the people really knew who you were without closed doors

They would not even have a desire to hear you anymore

Instead they would take a detour

Turn and start running to the opposite direction looking for the nearest corridor out to the exit door.

I don't question your anointing not your spiritual ability

Nor do I doubt oratorical capabilities

But I more concerned about that fact that you love the glitter, the glamour, and the hoopla more than you like the responsibility.

And trust me, you're not fooling nobody but yourself putting on a facade of modesty exemplifying fictitious humility.

You have become the hottest artist of the night

And you love to hear the people say

that you were the beast that ripped up the mic

And I personally don't mind saying that your lyrics are tight

but the problem is that not one soul has come to Christ.

I know that the gift will make room for you

and you got the skills to pay the bills

But what good are these skills if the heart is not being mended

and the soul is not being healed

Your pride has uncontrollably gotten the best of you to the point where it cannot be concealed

Your vocabulary is extensive but insubstantial

because of your inability to keep it real

Because if you are constantly speaking words

and your words are not helping anybody then your skills are nil!

You have become the biggest ticket town

But in the spirit realm you are a sub-par statistic.

Showing no signs of being altruistic

Do you even have the heart to spit this

It's obvious you can't handle the harsh linguistics

You truth is part holistic

And now lusting after your own vanity and

Spitting with no mental sanity

Your personality is subjectively narcissistic

Mad because you're not getting all of the

Finger snaps, hand claps, pats of the back and hand daps

Someone has stole your spotlight

You think something is wrong with that

You're too grown for that man!!!

Too busy looking for people to call you anointed

Pouting as if you're the only one that's appointed

So obsessed with putting on a good show

Your pride led you to become disfigured and disjointed

From the body you have become a spiritual disappointment.

If you're lacking substance then your ministry is pointless

Instead seeking the God of this

You seek public eminence

Without realizing the cost of it

Instead ministering the gift

You're content with flossin' it.

Rick Rossin it, forget about God

You rather be the boss of it.

And cost of this is humility

You have become dictatorial dogmatist

Beating your own chest

Like you took up the cross and went

To Calvary, to die and then purchased and bought the gift.

Now who's really the narcissist?

What profits a man to gain the whole world

At expense of his own soul And then become lost in it.

Your words are excitable but it lacks sincerity

Your delivery is impeccable but terribly your lifestyle lacks integrity

It seems like your pedigree is that of a Pharisee

Twisting biblical truths to increase your own celebrity

Presently it may appear to look heavenly

But the discrepancy is spiritual peasantry

Having no biblical equity, a short-lived ministry without the possibility of longevity,

But it is gradually deteriorating effectively and decrepitly

Making the people believe that it's Christ that you proclaim

Trying to give recognition to your so-called big name

Taking the name of the Lord God Jehovah in vain

Using the gift to turn tricks and run game

Putting on ministry to shame

And soon as you fall on your face

You looking for everybody but yourself to blame,

Because instead of trying to save souls

You're only looking to shine in these ten to fifteen minutes of fame.

Letting your gift to take you

Where your character cannot keep you

But the people can see through

The fake modesty and are able to see you

Trying to please you

You speak articulately

And your voice projects with clarity

So it's hard to see the intricacies

Because your words lack vulgarity

Vociferously boasting an arrogant mentality

Conspicuously becoming a sanctimonious whore

Prostituting yourself for the sake of popularity

You cannot serve two masters

And on this day you'll have to decide

And ask yourself the question of

Where does your soul reside?

Is it in God or world?

For one shall be worshipped and the other shall be denied

Because attitude will continue to consume you

Unless your ego begins to subside

FAKE HUMILITY

Jeremiah 17:9-10

Amplified Bible (AMP)

[9] The heart is deceitful above all things, and it is exceedingly perverse and corrupt and severely, mortally sick! Who can know it [perceive, understand, be acquainted with his own heart and mind]?

[10] I the Lord search the mind, I try the heart, even to give to every man according to his ways, according to the fruit of his doings.

Let me start this off by saying my heart is jacked up!! The King James version uses the term "desperately wicked"! I wanted to spend some extra time dealing with this issue, because many of us have become "churchy" as it relates to how we should behave. For example, when we come to service on Sundays, we act a certain way, as if everything is okay. Most of us are trained to say such things as, "I'm blessed and highly favored of the Lord," "The Lord is worthy to be praised," etc. We have been trained to some degree to say things we don't mean.

Although I verbalized "to God be the glory," I was still pounding my chest internally. I was too busy trying to be the hot act of the night or being the biggest draw, and I was too selfish to share the spotlight. I had to act like and look like I cared. I was jealous of other artists getting more applause than me. It's very painful to write this; hurtful to admit, but nonetheless true. I guess I'll be the lone sacrificial lamb in this one. This was and still is one hell of a fight. I was shaking hands and giving compliments to other artist who I thought were better than me because they deserved it. But I was still jealous on the inside that their ovation was better than mine. I was turning down smaller events for what I considered to be more prestigious events, or events that would get me more exposure. While I was still doing small events, I desired the bigger events or the events that would make me famous. I began to lose the focus of why I had this gift in the first place. This is an ongoing struggle and it's very hard not to straddle the fence with this.

I began to think that in taking these smaller events, I was doing them a favor. I was saying and doing all of the right things, but my heart was doing the total opposite. Just because we do the work of God as artists and poets does not mean that God is pleased, especially when our hearts are in the wrong place. My heart was and sometimes still is in the wrong place. Most often times, I'm able to catch it and repent of being this way. Sometimes I catch it and still do nothing about it. I have prayed on many occasions for God to take this away from me or take this ministry away from me. However, as my sister in the ministry, Jackie Hill Perry stated, I don't think that God takes away the struggle or the temptation, but He gives us the power to withstand them, flee from them, or overcome them. I completely agree with that statement and have not seen in scripture where God takes the temptations away from us. The scripture is very clear in mentioning this false sense of humility.

Jesus says that there will people who have done wonderful works, prophesied in His name, and cast out devils. But nevertheless He will profess to them, "I never knew you," and say to depart from Him, those who work in iniquity. Can you really hear what Jesus is saying in this? Let's break this down. There are people right now, as I speak, who are doing the work of God. There are people who are preaching God's word. There are people who prophesy and pray in Jesus. This means, in my own perspective, that there are people who benefit from the works of God, and who have prospered in the things of this world for the sake of Jesus' name, who will not enter into the kingdom of heaven.

It doesn't matter how anointed you may appear to be. It doesn't matter how popular a person may get or how many people come out to see you. Not everyone who says, "Lord, Lord," will enter into the kingdom of heaven. It doesn't even matter if someone else is getting delivered from your ministry. If someone has been delivered or healed from a song, poem, sermon, a book you wrote, or from laying hands on them, it is only because God used you to do it. It has absolutely nothing to do with you, me or anyone who has been called by God. So please understand, just because God has used you, doesn't necessarily mean that He knew you! Just because I'm used does not mean that I am approved. This is why ALL of the glory belongs to Him when it comes to others being delivered. If He used Satan to try Job, why would He not use a senseless, selfish, egotistical, pride-driven fool like me (Matthew 7:20-22)! I'm breaking down every stronghold today. He uses the FOOLISH things of this world to confound the wise!

Don't get it twisted. If you're in ministry and your heart is in the wrong place, God will still use you. But that will not constitute a personal relationship with Him. To keep your heart in the right place is a daily fight. You can't take any days off! There are people who try to justify themselves by saying, "God knows my heart." This is true, but the question is: Do you know your own heart? That answer would be an astounding *no*. I realized that I found pleasure in pleasing the crowd for applause and using God to accomplish that feat. God was surely not pleased with my false sense of humility.

PEOPLE PLEASING

Brene Brown mentioned in her book, the *Gifts of Imperfection,* (I'm paraphrasing a little) that "when we spend a lifetime trying to distance ourselves from the parts of our lives that do not fit in with who we think we're supposed to be, as a result, we stand outside of our own stories and we 'HUSTLE FOR WORTHINESS' by constantly performing, perfecting, pleasing, proving, and pretending to be someone we're not."

Man! This book is becoming more difficult to write as it progresses. This is probably one of my current struggles to date. I have always been a people pleaser as long as I can remember. Some struggles, I picked up over the years, but people pleasing was and still is a struggle. People pleasing or having the disease to please, in my opinion, is the overwhelmingly obsessive desire to get people to like or love you, no matter the cost -- usually at the expense of one's own happiness. It is a self-centered obsession, not to be well-respected but to be well-liked and accepted by everyone.

I call it self-centered because the focus is on self. Other people may not see it that way, because people pleasers are going out of their way to be there for others. It's hard to detect because there's a deeper objective for the people pleaser. The objective becomes subjective, whereas the people pleaser is more concerned about how the person feels about them rather than how he or she (the people pleaser) feels about the person. It took me a while to realize that I was being selfish as a people pleaser, because I always felt disappointed and sad if I couldn't please that person.

However, I realized that I was stressing because I wanted that deeper satisfaction of knowing that this person liked me. I used to think that I was being taken advantage of at times, when I would go out of my way to do things for people. But I wasn't doing this for them. I was actually doing this for me. I needed people to need me. Wow!

Okay, let me put it another way. For me to be satisfied with pleasing people, I considered it a necessity for them to have a need for me to be there for them. I needed them to need me like I needed air to breathe. It was almost a way of life for me. Although I was getting much satisfaction from this, it was also very draining. The pleasure that I got out of it was the attention that came from it. When I really looked deeper into this issue, I discovered that I was only doing this for attention, and not because I was a giving person. Yes, a giving person and a people pleaser are completely different people, in my opinion. However, it only appears that there are some similarities.

For example, the giving aspects of these two individuals are on completely different levels. The people pleaser is doing this for what they can get out of it. The giver is doing this for what God can get out it, and not wanting anything in return. The heart of the giver is selfless! The heart of the people pleaser is selfish. Some may not agree with me, but this is who I was as a people pleaser. Being a people pleaser was self-satisfying and self-gratifying for me. At one point in my life, I didn't agree with this principle, either. I actually despised the notion that I was a selfish person and I fought this for quite a long time. I also despised the person who told me I was selfish. Nobody could tell me I was selfish!

It's not that I *couldn't* say no to people, it's that I *wouldn't* say no to people. I once mentioned in a Facebook post that good deeds and acts of kindness do not necessarily determine what's on a person's heart. Yes, I did give to people, but I was grudging the cost. If I didn't get a good enough response from the people I did for, I would be disappointed in them. I would also never let them forget all of the things I had done for them. I did this intentionally to make them feel bad for not thanking me in the way I felt they should've thanked me.

I will submit this to the reader. Please be careful of the person who gives and does things for you with a grudging heart or a heart of self-seeking gratification. The main objective for me was based on what I could get from this. This is very difficult to write about because I'm talking about me. I can't speak for any other people pleaser, but I can tell you that I enjoyed holding people captive in situations because I would bring up the many things I did for them. I realized at a critical point in my life, that this could be very addictive, and I was taking advantage of people more than they would have taken advantage of me.

Also, at this critical stage, I realized my life had to change because this started to affect how I ministered to people in doing spoken word. Even in ministry, I began to perform for the sole purpose of trying to please people and get the right response or reaction. If I didn't get enough applause or standing ovation from the crowd, it wasn't a success in my eyes. The people pleasing spirit is a very dangerous spirit to pick up because it takes away the capacity to please God. This ultimately served as a deterrent from pleasing God. I was more concerned about what people thought of me than what God thought of me. At the expense of God's displeasure, I was pleasing people.

Please hear me, reader: If you want to truly please God, you have to stop trying to please people all the time! I simply did not care what God was thinking. That's a very dangerous place to be in, especially when you become so comfortable in the pleasure of people that you miss God. As a minister of God, and having a passion for people, I think that sometimes our passions are shifted to the cares of other people so much that it takes us away from caring for the things of God. I soon discovered, though genuine, I began to care for the things of the flesh, and one of the things that are of the flesh is over-indulging in the wants and desires of people, which distracts us from the wants and the desires of God.

One of the other things that made me a people pleaser was that I always felt undeserving. I would always turn down help from others. I always thought less of myself. So I will submit to the reader that it's okay to be selfless, but it's not okay to think less of yourself, especially when God neither sees nor thinks of you in that away. I want to be clear in this book. This is an attempt to help the believers and non-believers alike to be delivered from their bondage. We will never be freed from who we are if we never acknowledge who we are or what we have become. This had gotten so bad for me that it began to boil over into relationships. I was flattered by the attention that I got from women, particularly when I got into spoken word back in the 2003 to 2005 period. In that need to please, the response I got from women was overwhelming.

LOVING WOMEN

This is where people pleasing got me into trouble. Please understand that it is impossible to please everybody. I'll say it again: There's no way possible to please everybody. It is inevitable that someone will walk away from you disappointed. I tried to take this people pleasing spirit into pleasing women. Although this was very flattering to get this kind of attention from women, it would ultimately be to my detriment, as I was in multiple relationships at the same time. Now, some may say I was a low down dirty dog, a whore, trifling, irresponsible and I can't and won't argue with that. It is what it is. Some may say that because I didn't have a father in my life (who has too many children that it's hard to count), my trifling ways was inherited from him. Or that I was spoiled rotten by my grandmother and I was constantly looking for women to fill that void by going from woman to woman who would possess at least one of my grandmother's characteristics. Or, that I had an incredibly large ego and need more than one woman to stroke my ego. All those are valid points, and I won't argue with them either.

However, when you have a deeper need to please people, that will show up first before any of those other characteristics show up. I didn't necessarily get into these relationships because I liked the person. I got into these relationships because I liked how I was able to impress them with my conversation and intellect. I've heard many women say that nothing is more attractive than a man who is intelligent and can hold a very intriguing and stimulating conversation. So as a result, I was in relationships where I wasn't happy at all, but found it to be self-gratifying to be

90

loved by these women. I was never in love with any of these women, I was in love with pleasing them, even at the expense of my own happiness. And of course, I was satisfying my flesh in the process.

Now do you see how this can be dangerous? I was more concerned about pleasing people than my own happiness. I didn't care about being happy. Can't you see how sickening this can be? I was in it for the wrong reasons! This was one of the main reasons why I have two children out of wedlock. I was obviously trying to please more than one woman at a time. As it turned out, both of the women got pregnant. As a result, I have two children born in the same year; my son in February and my daughter in March. Both are the same age and exactly one month apart. Was I a dog? Yes! Was I trifling? Of course I was! But what I'm trying to get the reader to understand is that these roots run in a much deeper place other than my trifling proclivities.

I have a brother who I am very dear friends with, dealing with this same issue. I've known him all of my life. We talk quite often about having this people pleasing spirit. He ultimately married for this same reason. He didn't marry because he was happy. He married because this was pleasing to the person he was married to. As a result, he feels stuck in a marriage that he never wanted to be in, because his happiness was substituted for trying to please someone else. He married to make his wife happy at the expense of his own happiness. Due to the relationship he had with his in-laws, he also married to please his in-laws. He was actually in love with one person and let go of his own happiness because of the fear of what others would think of him, like his in-laws would.

In a deeper sense, people pleasers really have a need to be loved, and they think by doing things for others it will earn them the love they desire. The stress that comes with pleasing people can be very gut-wrenching, because when you try to please so many people at the same time, someone is sure to be disappointed.

I have come to the conclusion that I can only please one person at a time, so I'll start by pleasing God first and myself second, and whoever comes in the other spots, I'll deal with it accordingly. I've come to realize if you're trying to please ten people at one time, nine of them will suffer some kind of disappointment.

THE GIVER VS. THE PEOPLE PLEASER

This topic used to be very perplexing for me, simply because I never thought there was a difference. With that being said, there are many people pleasers who don't know the difference. It was and still is a very painful process in writing about this. However, if we're ever going to be free from our self-imposed prisons that we obviously confine ourselves to, we must confess our flaws and subject ourselves to complete admission of who we are, and our transparency must take center stage.

The people pleaser gives with the specific intent of expecting something in return, whether it is money, time, availability, affection, or even friendship. The giving person gives with a pure heart. They don't have any hidden motives, agendas, or any expectancies. Life coach Vickie Champion says that people pleasers are more apt to give only with the expectation of getting. From a deeper perspective, the people pleaser is convinced that doing things for others is a down payment for something they'll get in return. They often times expect to be rewarded. However, in a real sense, they're expecting compensation for their so-called acts of kindness. They expected to be appreciated. They want high praise and honor or some kind of security. The giver does not care for personal praise or any honor, because he or she understands that their honor comes from God.

The giver cares about the things of God and family. The people pleaser care about things of other people even at the expense of family negligence. That's right. Some people pleasers will neglect the very ones who love them the most to please someone they hardly know. The people they're trying to please probably don't care about them, one way or the other. The giver is truthful. The people pleaser will lie to avoid conflict or to keep someone's friendship. They will often times tell a person what they want to hear to avoid hurting their feelings. However, the giver carefully considers the person's feelings before responding in an appropriate, precise, and orderly manner. Last but absolutely not the least, the people pleaser tries their best to fix everyone else's lives, but has minimal interest in rectifying their own. The giver is interested in fixing their own lives and is a walking example of how others should fix theirs.

I was, and in some instances still am, a people pleaser. But I am working diligently in my deliverance to be better. But I must inform you people pleaser who's reading this book. You have to come clean!! You have to stop hiding behind this mask of having it all together. You have to be able to exploit yourself. If you really want to help yourself and others, come clean today. I wrote a poem called "Brokenness" a few years back to cope with the mentality of pleasing people and the depression that can come along with it.

BROKENNESS

Psalm 51:17

Amplified Bible (AMP)

[17] My sacrifice [the sacrifice acceptable] to God is a broken spirit; a broken and a contrite heart [broken down with sorrow for sin and humbly and thoroughly penitent], such, O God, You will not despise

Out of the depths of despair, depression, and hopelessness.

I speak in brokenness

And every single time I am faced with a situation

I write to find the best way of approaching this

So through spoken lips

I must verbally vent and express my ongoing frustration of how to cope with this.

So with boldness and clarity

I will openly discuss and exploit my disparity

Because there are things in my life that I'm going through that I don't care to be

But are necessary even though sometimes

it just doesn't seem quite fair to me.

So as I attempt to pluck up

the root of my trials, tribulations and my misery

Please understand that I have been hurt by some of

the very folk I considered near and dear to me

And it has become painfully obvious and quite clear to me.

That everything is not always what they appear to be.

Are you hearing me?

You see the scripture says guard your heart with all diligence

For out of it flow the issues of life.

So I have to protect my heart

because I don't know what you will

Think of me when I step away from

this platform at the end of the night.

Because when I leave this place there will be some issues that are

Waiting on me at home that I'll have to fight.

Whatever goes on in the darkness will surely come to the light.

And tonight

My question is do you know what's behind this mic...

Sleepless nights, loss of appetites

Broken spirits, hearts contrite.

Struggling to make ends meet, going home to no lights

One failed relationship after another ending in bitterness and strife.

Constant thoughts of death, having neither cause nor reason to continue in life.

I had no motivation

I lost the passion to do things that I love the most, I was void of inspiration.

It got to the point where I was no longer motivated to speak my voice

I was no more than the walking dead, solitarily confined

To a cemetery of my own choice

My spirit was crushed, my bones were frozen, my soul was cold.

I was stressing out over situations

that were far out of my reach and beyond my control.

Excessively overeating and gaining unnecessary weight

Allowing other people to determine and dictate to me my own fate

And most of time these situations have me bent out of shape.

And I have finally found out how to get away and take a break

And now poetry has become my way of escape.

So as I stand on this platform, this is how I keep my sanity

And this is an avenue to release my grievous afflictions and destructive calamities

Because these cuts, wounds and scars that are on the inside of me have become infected and have proven to be severely damaging.

I don't think you're understanding me.

Pain is inevitable and no one is ever exempt from this

And sometimes poetry is the only sane and therapeutic way.

For me to be fulfilled and replenished of my emptiness.

There were pivotal moments in my life

that were ever so delicate and significantly vital.

I was beginning to lose every sense of intellect,

My emotions began to over cloud my judgment and my thoughts became suicidal.

You see I would always brush my problems to the side, sweep it under the rug,

Suppressing the issues and dealing with other people's problems

At the expense of my own leisure

I felt if I would continue to indulge myself in other people's affairs.

They would like me more, but it became even more stressful to be a people pleaser.

I gave up so much of myself to please people to the point where

My future no longer looked promising.

My heart could no longer handle the overflowing capacity

Of issues I was putting inside of it, I was emotionally and psychologically vomiting.

Thinking, that if I would just jump into another relationship and have

My lil boo on the side that it would take all of my hurt away.

But that only created more problems because all of the pain

From past relationships resurfaced, and it began to regurgitate.

Never allowing myself time to heal

Viciously repeating the same cycle to hide my pain and I knew,

How low and degrading it would make me feel.

These situations began to stress me out so much that it started

To take a toll on my physical being.

I was stepping outside of my own character to be there

For other people who didn't give a damn about my well being.

Yes I was so devastated and distraught my body was beginning to pay the cost.

Sometimes I would lie down and sleep for eight hours straight

And still wake up tired and overwhelmed with exhaustion.

I began to experience pain in my gut, neck, back, legs, chest, and

Other parts of my body I'd rather not say.

And if you don't learn from your situations, your

Body and mind will continue to have a harsh price to pay.

You see it only takes one event to turn your whole life around

As long as you continue to give heed to a dead unchanging situation

It will persist to keep you bound.

Which will ultimately result in an internal cataclysmic breakdown.

In laymen's terms, you will become a basket case

My brothers and sisters, you have to let it go before it's too late.

Depression is an only seed

And it does not discriminate on the basis of how big or small

A situation may be, it is how the situation is perceived.

So you should be careful not to belittle someone else

Because you feel like their issues are too small for them to be upset.

Because you can be dealing with Hurricane Katrina and you can be

Dealing with a thunderstorm and it can still have the same effect.

The seed of depression only gives false hope, distorted reasoning,

And the wrong kind of encouragement.

Low self-esteem, fear, worry, unbelief, doubt, and worthlessness

Are the elements that provide the seed its nourishment.

Believe me when I tell you that outcome of your depression will not be pretty.

And if you're not careful you will literally begin

To choke and drown in the sea of your own self-pity.

You have to make sure that you stay away from the issue

That GOD has allowed you to overcome.

Because it's amazing how some of us have a crippling tendency

To revert back to the very thing that GOD delivered us from.

I'm not here to entertain

I'm here to bless you.

I'm trying to help ease some of your pain

Help break the psychological chains.

And I have killed the man that has tried to impress you.

My brothers and sisters, let it go and allow GOD to heal you.

Because if you continue to allow this junk to grow inside of you,

The depression will literally kill you.

Find the truth, know the truth, and let it set you free.

And if this ain't helping nobody, then surely it's helping me.

Sometimes I have to speak to these spirits and call them out by name

Reproaches, infirmities, and necessities,

For when I am weak, CHRIST is strong,

And the enemy won't ever get the best of me.

Surrender yourself unto GOD and subject yourselves to truth, honesty and openness.

Because GOD is and always will be in the habit of showing Himself strong

In the midst of your brokenness.

Unfortunately, people pleasers attract other people pleasers. They will always try to outdo each other. Some people feel the need to control everything around them, and some people pleasers will allow themselves to be controlled. I was never the controlling type. However, I did allow people to control me for the simple reason of making them feel good about themselves.

This obviously spilled over into many failed relationships that I've been in, where sex ruled the

103

relationship from start to finish. It seemed like the only time we got along was in the bedroom, which was very unhealthy and unstable. At any rate, sex controlled me and I got into unhealthy relationships just because I thought the sex was good. While the sex was good, the relationships always got progressively worse. Sex was only a distraction and I was hooked. I love my children to death, and I am very fortunate to have them in my life. But it is very unfortunate that they were a result of poor choices and poor decision making. I wouldn't trade my kids for the world or anything in it, but their dad was very trifling in doing the very things the Bible asks us not to do. This is something that I live with every day of my life. Both of my children are now eight years old. I never wanted to be labeled as a "baby daddy," but this is the bed I made, so I have to lie in it.

These life experiences (people-pleasing, sex, lying, failed relationships) caused me to fall into a very deep stage of depression. So I had to stop hiding behind the mask of joy and happiness when hurt, pain, anger, and depression were living a private life behind it. As men, we are not particularly good at expressing how we feel, especially when it comes to *explaining* how we feel and trying to verbalize our emotions. So poetry was the only thing I found that could help me with expressing myself. Even though I have become very good at expressing myself, not just through poetry but even in my own everyday life, it is still very painful to deal with my emotions, even as I write this book. The fear of being called soft or being called a punk still resonates within me today. But poetry is the substratum, the foundation, or undergirding of how I deal with these fears. Poetry is also the strategy that enables me to take off the mask and come from behind the veil.

Behind The Veil

I'm going through something because I'm sitting up late
at night,

Brainstorming trying to find the proper antidote for all

these demons I'm trying to fight,

And it's getting kind of tight,

Because I'm trying to find my own way through the
darkness

Without calling on GOD for any spiritual insight,

I'm in a serious predicament and I hope that you'll feel
my plight,

Because I'm thinking to myself if I get married, then

I would be able to make things right

But it would be foolish for me to do this thing out of spite

And deliberately marry the wrong woman

just to cure my perverted sexual appetite

Am I marrying the booty or

Am I marrying my wife?

And it seems like, I'm putting up a fuss

Trying to justify my reasons for sheltering

these categorical demons of lust,

And it's an extreme disgust,

Plus I must,

Admit,

That fornication is one of the biggest demons I've had to wrestle with,

And this particular demon has been overwhelmingly difficult to tussle with

In the midst of the hustle and bustle and this gift,

That GOD has given me to spit

That has absolutely nothing to do with

The fact that I'm spiritually sick,

And my soul.......needs to be fixed!

Because right now it feels like my soul

is broken beyond repair

But tonight I am prepared,

To go deep into the very depths and the most intricate parts of my inner being,

Forgive me y'all, but I think I'm getting ready to go there,

Because it seems like I'm running away from the problem instead of facing the struggle

And instead of me trying to cast this thing away it seems like I'm embracing the struggle,

Because the reality,

Is that I wrestle against powers and principalities

Rulers of darkness, evil intentions and deceptive mentalities.

My battle is against evil spiritual wickedness in high places,

And these demons that I'm dealing with do not come in the form of a serpent

But they're fine, attractive, with big hips and cute faces, and sometimes I just want to

Throw in the towel and just quit

Because Satan will sometimes make a person look ten times better

Than the one you're supposed to be with

Because you see, my brothers and sisters, John says all that is in the world

The lust of the flesh, the lust of the eyes, the pride of life,

But my question is what am I supposed to do when so many things

Look pleasing to the very sight

Awwww man, I wish I could

See no evil,

And hear no evil,

Therefore I won't be able to

Speak no evil,

And do no evil.

Ya see, I kinda feel like Paul

because the very things that I hate

those are the very things that I do

and when I will to do the things that are right

those are the very things that I don't do

and I'm sitting there wondering why I'm committing

all these lustful acts over and over and over again.

But you see it's not really the act, but Solomon says it is

The very thought of foolishness that makes it a sin.

And on that same note James says that lust when it has been

Conceived by the thoughts it brings forth sin,

And eventually when the sin is full grown it brings forth death,

Not from a physical perspective, but ultimately death from within.

And now my sins are on a constant incline,

Because I've come to realize that it is merely a sin once you have

Conceptualized the thought of doing it in your mind

I'm entertaining ungodly thoughts and vain imaginations, and

I'm sick and tired of the same obstacles, trials and tribulations.

And now my mind is being overwhelmed by an excessive amount of skepticism,

because I'm dealing with demonic forces and these unruly damnable despotisms.

And yes I'm a Christian and yes I'm saved, but I'm not gon front like church folk,

And act like I got it all together when I bring my sins to the altar,

Because some of these so-called church folk can be some of the biggest

Hypocrites the world has to offer.

That's why I can't look down on other people because to me I have to be self-scorning,

because I'm fantasizing about the demons 2, 3, 4, and 5 o'clock in the morning.

I so desperately want to get rid of this thing but I am constantly yearning

Every time I try to suppress it, it keeps returning

I know the scripture says it is better to marry than to burn

But the question of conviction (sexually concerning) the flesh that resonates in my mind keeps on confirming

What happens when you get married and you're still burning?

Sometimes the flesh, it feels so good that I don't even want to get rid of the sin

And I'm thinking to myself, Lord, how can I win,

If I'm beginning to neglect my own spirit and find comfort in the sin that I'm living in.

And it almost feels like I'm in a state of contentment

And on top if all that I'm dealing with anger, pride, lying, procrastination,

Jealousy, selfishness, and resentment.

And now there's an increased depression in my expression, stressing, because I'm dealing with this abnormal behavior and this compulsive obsession.

I'm just about a block away from trifling but I choose to walk in the other direction

It almost reminds me of the story of Legion

And I have all these lustful thoughts lingering in my mind and I'm screaming,

Lord Jesus, help me, save me from this spiritual crack addiction 'cause I'm fiending,

Even, in a deep sleep I'm dreaming,

And now I'm losing my own sanity and I'm beginning to hallucinate about these demons,

And I can hear 'em calling, and calling, and calling and calling.

Constantly while I'm falling, and falling, and falling, and falling.

And it seems like the more I walk steadfastly in the will of GOD,

Instead of prospering I'm suffering

I'm going to church every Sunday, Bible study every Wednesday, praying three times a day, reading my Bible, paying my tithes and I'm still struggling

And even though I'm going through this particular thing, I try my best not to show it.

Because subconsciously you can be addicted to the drama that you're going through in your

Own life and still not even know it.

And sometimes I get so discouraged I feel like I will never get delivered

From these weaknesses that I have

But my question is, have I been prone to do these things

dating back to my generational past.

Because this is something that I struggle with every single day

And these demons don't want me to tell the truth

But I'm telling the truth anyway

'Cause it seems like GOD has taken his hand away from me and HE has forgotten me

It makes me want to throw up my hands and shout out Eli, Eli, Lama Sabachthani.

But I'm not JESUS and I cannot even begin to compare myself to the ONE who

Died to save a wretched man like me, thank You, LORD!

But believe me when I say that this spiritual walk with GOD is hard!

You don't hear what I'm saying to you, I've been going through this thing for far too long and

I'm ready to call these demons out

Do you understand the words that are coming out of my mouth.

Because I'm tired, y'all!

I really don't know how much more I can take.

It feels like I'm in the solitary confinements of my own thinking capacity for GOD's sake

And this is my debate,

Do I have time to make

Things right and rectify the situation before it's too late

Because it seems like I'm running out of time,

And I'm looking for some kind,

Of supernatural sign,

To get me out of this spiritual bind,

Because I have become a prisoner of my own mind.

And it's demoralizing to try as hard as you can to do what is right and still fail.

It's kind of like doing all that you can to get out of jail but you still can't make bail

And because my mind has become so increasingly frail,

I have to humble myself, exploit who I am,

And go Behind the Veil.

I have to strip myself of these fig leaves

I cannot continue to hide

I can no longer stand here and tell you a lie

So in order to rid myself of these fleshly things I must be willing to die

Because right now I'm so filthy and dirty in the eyes God

It feels like the garbage in a trash can,

So I have to make sure that I go boldly behind the veil so

You won't have to ask who was that masked man

Behind the veil!

I want to be able to minister to the inner you

But before I do that I must humble myself and admit that I am a sinner too

Behind the Veil

I have to make sure that God's will is being done

But before I do that I have to stop hiding behind GFSoldier

And introduce you to Hilton Christopher Young.

114

THE MASK OF CHRISTIANITY

Mark 7:5-9

(The Message)

Jesus answered and said: Isaiah was right when he prophesied about frauds like you. Hit the bull's eye in fact. These people make a big show of saying all of the right things but their heart is not in it. They act like their worshipping me but they really don't mean it. They just use me as a cover-up to teach whatever suits their fancy; ditching God's command and taking up the latest fads. Well good for you. You get rid of God's command so that you won't be inconvenienced in following your own religious fashion.

I must submit this to the people pleaser who's reading this book. You are NOT making things better for yourself or the person(s) you're trying to please. You have to start considering the long-term effect that this can cause! More than anything, I grew very tired of putting on the façade of Mr. Goody Two-Shoes. I became exhausted from being the dumpster and allowing everybody and their dog to dump or empty their garbage on me. I was very agitated and frustrated with myself that I put my life on hold for everybody. I was tired of neglecting my loved ones for the sake of trying to please someone who really didn't give a damn about me. I was tired of losing friends who walked away from me because they couldn't get what they wanted out of me.

It was becoming too expensive to keep up this fast-paced tempo of trying to please everybody. The time was too expensive. The energy was too expensive, and the money was also too expensive. I got tired of being everybody's doormat. I was so engulfed in trying to please everybody else that I forgot to give God what He rightfully deserved. Pleasing people became more important to me than pleasing God. I got tired of losing sleep, due to excessive worrying about what people thought of me because of something I did. I spent thirty-eight years of my life being there for everybody else and pleasing everybody else.

Now I'm working on the next thirty-eight years to please God and be there for myself. I got tired of looking like a good Christian, acting like a good Christian, and not *being* a Christian at all. I got extremely tired of faking it until I made it. Most of all, I got tired of abusing God's grace, mercy and forgiveness to justify everything I did. It is such a dangerous place to be when God's mercy is being used as an excuse to continue in the sin that you know full well is wrong. I tired of that as well. I got tired of raising my hands in church to make it look like I was in worship, when I was actually doing only what the worship leader was telling me to do. I got tired of going to events to be seen rather be heard. I got tired of being a PROSTITUTE claiming to be Christian.

Unfortunately, we're living in a day where many of us who call ourselves Christians are shamefully disgracing God's honor and are really giving "Christian" a bad name. We have in many ways lost the integrity of who we are in the body of Christ. We have to get back to being good examples of Christ's integrity. It is only through our integrity in God that we become better examples for the world to see. We have become very hypocritical in who we are as Christians.

When I wrote this poem I looked at myself in the mirror and I knew that I did a good job of acting like a Christian, but inside I was not being Christ-like at all. We as a church body have became very good at putting on the façade of knowing how to act in church but reverting back to our selfish ways as soon as the service lets out. This poem is for the corporate body to get our act together.

CHRISTIAN INTEGRITY

Three of the most loosely translated words

In the English diction

Is friend, love, and Christian

And it's crazy because my intuition

Gave me a funny feeling about

The response I would get on this one

When I first started out on this mission

I had a pretty good definition

Of the position that this particular word was given

The title that was given and the magnitude of provision

And excluding my own opinionated psychological cognition

I understood that its terms, policies, and conditions

Were a lot less concerned about the words that I speak

Scriptures I quote

Even constructing my own theological erudition

By allowing religion to make revisions

Of a Word that was written

Long before my existence was ever bored into fruition

But rather the intention focuses more of its attention

On the substantiated sufficiency

Of the lifestyle I'm living

How efficient is my ability to listen

To its true law instead of the deficiency

Of sanctimonious church traditions

Which in opposition

Subconsciously separate her doctrines, customs, practices, and dispositions

From the immaculacy of true biblical renditions

So my questions are

How deep is my submission to its requisition?

How accurate is persistence to its precision?

Will I elaborate my own salvation as an excuse to loosen integrity from its constriction? Do I follow its ordinances, precepts, and commissions?

Or do I abuse its consent, allowances, and permissions?

Do I use this as tool to popularize my own ambitions as poet, artist, rhetorician, speaker, teacher, academician?

Do I obey its ethics?

Or do I reject its prohibitions?

And when I do happen to fall

Does my heart subject itself to true brokenness and contrition?

Or will I bastardize God's grace????

As justification or trying to be Christ-like

And hypocrite in juxtaposition

Without exercising any iniquitous dereliction

Monopolizing His forgiveness a get out of jail free card sin remission

So there's no way that I can be exempt from this interdiction

And act as though I have divine jurisdiction

To hand out these harsh admonitions

When this particular Word's convictions

Obligate me to look in the mirror

And rid myself of these bigoted premonitions

And realize that the criterion of its restrictions

Prevents me from looking down on someone else

With my own accusations and unreasonable suspicions

And come into the full admission

That if I toot my nose at someone else

As if they are inferior with my own condescending depictions

I have perverted, corrupted, and have taken

Sincere irrevocable purity away from the word Christian

Now who is it that are among you that can really say that they are Christian?

Who can really say that they love Christ?

Especially if you are boldly professing to be

What your heart does not possess you to be

Aggressively, tell people that they're going to hell

If they do not properly confess to be

"CHRISTIAN"

Making yourself to be the kind of person

That comes to church on Sunday

And leave without showing in implications of the effects

That it has on you from Monday

Through Saturday

It seems like your former day

Does not solicit you to change in these latter days

As long as you come to church

You don't feel the need to take heed to what the pastor says

So you decide to revise the script and ad lib the role like the actor plays

Using Christianity to cover up your filth like a masquerade

And it appears as though this type of fraudulence

Has accumulated a mass crusade

Of people who have become good at faking it until they make it

So that they can get all the glory the honor and the accolade

When a lost soul comes to church you set up a barricade

Because you feel like the person doesn't look right

Well can somebody tell me what a Christian is supposed to look like?

All of a sudden I can get the invite

Because I don't appear to be the church-going type

However if I wanted to make a large contribution with my debit card

Would not think twice

About running to go get a mechanical device

Or an ATM to show me where I can swipe

It makes me wonder

Is Christianity all that it's cracked up to be?

Or is it a bunch of hype

I'm supposed to be a lamp that shine bright

In a dark world with blind sight

However in hindsight

If I continue to present myself deceptively claiming to be right

I am no more than the false disciple

Who transforms himself into an apostle of Christ

And no wonder

For Satan himself is able to transform into an angel of light

And it's so unfortunate that there's a disproportionate, metamorphosis, of people who call themselves Christians who are insubordinate, to God's ordinance. So when the unsaved come to church they're wondering is this really God's house or Satan's orphanage? Spiritually lynching the non-believers before they can become born again, we have become mass abortionists,

Abusing our authority by raising that extra, extra offering to get more of it, accepting excessive deposits to profit our pockets has got people thinking that we're prophets when are mentally extortionate; please forgive me if I seem to be a bit vitriolic; because

I believe in bringing in all the tithes and offerings into the store house

So that there can shelter for the homeless

Church funding, and food for the poorhouse

But it appears that ministry has become the new hustle

That's being birthed out of the Lord's house

Where the preachers are the pimps

The congregations are the prostitutes

And the sanctuary has become the whorehouse

And Jesus has become the new sales pitch

Totally undermining the nail prints in His nailed wrists

Just like Judas's betrayal kiss

Totally disrespecting the one who gave us the nostrils to inhale with

And it is only to my detriment

If I continue to display a self-indulging decadence

That will bring about a resonance

Of foolishness that will be made prevalent

To a people who always hear the proclamation of Christ

But constantly sees the negligence

They hear me talking about faith

But my actions contradict the evidence

So they sit back and observe me acting outside my own hypocritical element

Just as the mischievous child reverts back

To the old pattern of his own behavioral petulance

I am the dog that vomits and returns to consume its own excrement

And consider the word Christian

A word that was once esteemed to be highly revered

Is beginning to become more irrelevant

And my question to you ladies and gentlemen

While living in the midst of this violent land amuck

Will the real Christian please stand up??

CHALLENGING THE BODY OF CHRIST

I truly believe that the Body of Christ has to be challenged and start revealing who Christ is. We have become very hypocritical in being representatives, followers of Christ. Please forgive me, but I have to address this issue. The church in particular has possibly become the biggest hypocrite of our time. I am a part of this church, and as much as I love the church I also must be critical of her.

We have been persistently arguing against same-sex marriage, and I think this is very hypocritical of us the church to fight this thing. Now, don't get me wrong. I truly believe that homosexuality is flat out wrong; without the shadow of doubt. However, I also believe that lust and fornication are wrong also, and the church is negligently and dangerously ignoring it. We magnify the sin of homosexuality and are now putting the sin of homosexuality in lights as if the other hundreds of lustful sins recorded in the Bible don't exist. We (the church) are fostering more unmarried Christian couples than ever before. We are having families out of wedlock and the church isn't saying anything.

Jesus said, behold why are you trying to take the stick out of your brother's eye when you have a log in your own eye? First take the log out your own eye and you can see clearly to take the stick out of your brother's eye (Matthew 7:1-5). We as a corporate body have a very huge log in our eye and that log is blinding us from seeing the clear fact that we have to clean it up first if we want the world to clean it up! We cannot expect the world to be right if the church isn't right and until the church cleans up her act, I truly believe she should keep her mouth shut!!!

We have been quick to point the finger at what's going wrong in the world, but surely that won't stop the judgment that is due to us as a corporate body. Paul makes that evidently clear in saying that when we judge others, we immediately condemn ourselves. Somehow we have esteemed the sin of homosexuality above the other sins, as if it's much worse than fornication. Isn't homosexuality a form of fornication? Isn't it a form of lust? Paul clearly says that we (the church) are without excuse! Paul goes on to say that due to the fact that we commit sin, what makes us think that we can get away with the sin by pointing the finger at someone else (Romans 2:3)? How dare we!!!

How can we tell the world do not fornicate when we are fornicating? How can we tell the world don't lie, cheat, and steal when we who are supposed to be examples of Christ are doing the same things? Paul says, no wonder it is written that the Gentiles sin and blaspheme the name of God because you (Romans 2:24). We have set an extremely poor example of doing the will of God. We have dangerously become increasingly accepting of unmarried couples shacking up in the church, and the unmarried couples are in the church at an alarming rate!!

Now that the world wants to legalize homosexuality, we want to speak up? As filthy as we are, now we want to say something? Seriously? Whatever is going on in the world, we are partly responsible for where the world is now. I truly believe that the world looks at our example. Can we honestly say that we have been a good example for the world to see? Sin has become an obsolete topic to talk about, particularly in the area of fornication. However, the only sin we have made an exception for is homosexuality. Wow! How hypocritical is that?

Mahatma Ghandi who was a practicing Buddhist was once asked by a reporter whether or not he still rejected Christ. His response was no. "I love your Christ! I just don't love your Christians!" He went on to say that "your Christians are so unlike Christ." Mahatma Ghandi was born in the late 1800s and died in the late 1940s, and this is what he was saying about Christianity then. Have we gotten any better since then? We can neither forget nor ignore sin as if it no longer exists. We cannot teach about some sin and not talk about all of it, particularly as it pertains to lust and sex/fornication.

FORNICATION

Okay, so let's deal with this issue of fornication. If you're nasty and choosing to stay that way, then you probably don't want to read this section. However, if you're looking to gain more understanding, read on. At any rate, it seems like this is the number one issue that no one in the church wants to talk about, so let's roll with it. We are so caught up in teaching how to be blessed and how to prosper that we duck and dodge issues of this magnitude.

So let us look at the word fornication. It comes from the Greek language, "porneia," which is translated in English as porn or pornography. Many times we associate fornication with pre-marital sex, particularly in the area of intercourse. As long as the man does not penetrate, then it's not fornication. Many people, particularly Christians, believe this very concept, and I am certainly guilty of this philosophy myself. However, fornication is much more than pre-marital intercourse. Intercourse is often times the end result of most sexual activity. There are also other forms of sex or fornication, and the Bible alludes to them.

Paul makes a very bold statement to the Corinthian church in saying that it is not good for man to "touch" a woman! However to avoid fornication, let every man have his own wife and every woman have her own husband (1 Corinthians 7:1-2). It appears that Paul does not limit fornication to mere intercourse or penetration. But it seems as if Paul refers to fornication as certain types of touching. He clearly states that it is not good for a man to touch a woman. So it appears that this kind of touching could be oral sex, fondling of certain body parts, or even tongue kissing, depending on how one will interpret this particular passage of scripture. If tongue kissing stimulates you sexually (down there), then you may want to consider this because this type of kiss can also lead to other sexual activities. If there's any kind of touching that stimulates you sexually, and can possibly lead to other sexual activity, you may want to consider stopping.

NOBODY is that strong all of the time!!! You may resist it a few times. But the truth is, none of us are built to handle this particular temptation on our own. Remember, the scripture never said to resist fornication. It said to FLEE or run from it (1 Corinthians 6:18)! But it appears as if Paul is saying that all of this can be avoided if the man and the woman get married. I have been guilty of all of this. So those of you who think you're practicing celibacy because there's no penetration involved, you may want to re-think your philosophy on that. Just because there's no penetration doesn't mean that you're abstaining or celibate. Many people often use oral sex and other forms of sex as a substitute to keep the title of celibacy. There are also some who use oral sex and other forms of sex as mechanism to cure their urge, hunger, or appetite for intercourse, but that only enhances it.

Well, it appears that if you engage in a form of fornication where touching can be sexual, then you're no longer celibate. Grabbing someone's behind in a sensual way or touching a woman's breast can also be fornication, in accordance with what these verses appear to be saying. I know this is tough, but I want to make sure I don't leave anything out. We have to come into the fullness of truth as it relates to God if we want to be considered His followers and be good examples of Christ.

Now, let me be clear on this topic. This is only my interpretation of this topic. I'm not writing this for you to agree with me. If you don't agree, I totally understand. I would have fought against this concept myself a few years back. My resistance to this topic was the very reason I had children out of wedlock by two different women. It was only because I was able to die to myself and confess that I was trifling, irresponsible and nasty that today I am delivered from this. But it doesn't mean that the temptation to do it is not ever present.

This is why you have to die daily to stay delivered. You have to die daily because this is a daily struggle that most men who love women deal with. In my opinion, it's a natural innate instinct. This begs the question: How do I walk in a will that appears to go against the very nature in which I was born? Just because you were born into sin doesn't mean that it's okay to commit sin.

DEATH BY LETHAL INJECTION

This is probably one of the most difficult things that one will ever have to endure as a Christian, but it is quite rewarding, I must say. This topic comes from the analogy of a prisoner being on Death Row. When the defendant is sentenced to death by lethal injection, there's usually a waiting period before the person is actually put to death. It is said that due to the complexity of expensive time-consuming appeals, and procedures mandated in the jurisdiction, the wait for execution can be as long as fifteen years. Also there is a shortage of the lethal injection drug that takes time and money to produce.

Well, I must tell you, if you claim to be a Christian, then you must understand that this practice is a "daily death sentence." Also with the daily death sentence, we have an unlimited supply of lethal injection drug. That would be the Word of God. My good friend and co laborer in the artistry, Leonard "The Oracle" Woodard, has a song called "Lethal Injection Unlimited Supply." Although this song has been out for quite of few years, it just recently ministered to me. There's no waiting period on this daily death sentence. This lethal injection called the Word of God is the antidote of killing the flesh. Paul specifically talks about dying and facing death every day, when it comes to serving and fellowshipping with God (1 Corinthians 15:31).

This lethal injection is not inaccessible. It's not hard to come by. Everybody has access to it. The problem is that many of us don't want to die. When we come to Christianity, we want to continue to be who we are and not what God always intended for us to be. Those of us who are nasty want to continue to be nasty. We don't want to have to commit to someone for us to get some. We don't want to be married to continue to get sex when we want it. So we in turn learn enough Bible to be able to justify our trifling tendencies. I have also been guilty of this. I have been on both sides of this spectrum. I have engaged in very articulate and intelligent arguments to just be trifling. I was very good at making good intellectual points and using scripture to back up my point. I was good at taking a false argument and making it sound plausible. In theological debate, I would shut down people who were well versed in the scripture because of what I knew. Remember, Satan probably knows the scripture better than any of us. But God was definitely not pleased with me and allowed some things to happen in my life that gave me no other choice but to die spiritually.

So do understand there are only two ways that you will utilize the Word of God. You will either use it to do God's will or your own will. There's no in between. You will either die to your flesh and live in the spirit, or vice versa.

HOW THE GIFT SAVED MY LIFE?

Everything up to this point in the book is a testimony coupled with information on some of the things I had to do to allow the gift to work itself in me. Not only that, but to allow God to stir up the gift in me. I really took some time to understand what I was doing when I wrote and recited those P.O.E.M.s. I was completely unaware of the counseling I was receiving by merely writing my thoughts, feelings, and emotions down on paper and expressing them openly.

I realized that I was always able to speak in front of crowds and without hesitation or reluctance. I didn't understand the significance in writing a poem in the 6th grade and winning first place in the poetry contest; a poem that is still being used as the motto of that school today. I didn't understand the big deal about getting in front of a student body in elementary school and reciting a Langston Hughes poem I memorized the week before. What's crazy about that? That was one of my failing years, 7th grade. I was smart enough to memorize a poem and recite it in front of the entire student body, but couldn't pass the 7th grade. Wow!!

My teacher saw enough potential in me to recite a poem, but didn't believe I could pass the 7th grade. She often times embarrassed me in front of my classmates when I made bad grades, which really took shots at my self-esteem big time. Maybe she thought shaming me in front of my classmates would make me do better, but it actually made me do worse. Obviously I had a different learning style than most of my classmates, and instead of trying to exploit the strengths of my learning style, she exploited my weaknesses and made fun of me in front of everybody. Maybe it was an effort to try to bring out the best in me. We'll give her the benefit of the doubt.

I didn't see a future in doing this when I memorized the "Mountain Top" sermon/speech written by our Drum Major for Justice, the Reverend Dr. Martin Luther King, Jr. in high school, and recited it in front of the student body. I also did perform poorly in the classroom. I had to go to summer school each of my five years in high school to get promoted to the next grade and graduate. I didn't understand that when I won the talent portion of the Mr. Iowa Central Contest in college, by writing my own speech, and barely kept a 2.2 GPA that I would be doing this. I couldn't possibly fathom at the time why the president of that college would fly me all the way back from Louisiana to Iowa to the graduation ceremony to be the commencement speaker, and I was nowhere near the top of the class, grade-wise. Although I was playing football at my four-year college, I didn't comprehend the importance of being called "Mr. Bible Study." I didn't understand how I began to take such a keen and genuine interest in studying the Bible while sporting a 1.9 GPA.

My point in saying all this and reiterating this is negligence. I was neglecting my gift. I never looked at it as being a gift, but more of a hobby or a pastime. I never took it seriously until more people began to request me to be a speaker/poet at their events; until I started to be mentioned amongst some of the best poets in the nation. I didn't understand it until people, young and old, started asking me to mentor them, teach at their seminars, and conduct workshops as a facilitator.

If people were to tell my story, I was not supposed to be here. It baffled me that this whole time, I was neglecting my gift. Paul is real clear on not neglecting the gift.

1 Timothy 4:12-16

12. Do not let anyone despise or think less of you because of your youth, but be an example (pattern) for the believers in speech, in conduct, in love, in faith, and in purity.

13. Till I come, devote yourself to [public and private] reading, to exhortation (preaching and personal appeals), and to teaching and instilling doctrine.

14. Do not neglect the gift which is in you, [that special inward endowment] which was directly imparted to you [by the Holy Spirit] by prophetic utterance when the elders laid their hands upon you [at your ordination].

15. Practice and cultivate and meditate upon these duties; throw yourself wholly into them [as your ministry] so that your progress may be made evident to everybody.

16. Look well to yourself [to your own personality] and to [your] teaching; persevere in these things [hold to them], for by so doing you will save both yourself and those who hear you.

SHAKE OFF THE HATERS

Parents!!! This is especially for you and the kids you're raising. Although this applies to everyone who reads this book, I want to focus on the young people and the parents who raise them. If your kids are not doing as well as you think they should, for whatever reason, please understand that there's a deeper purpose that's going on inside of your children. Usually the child who does the poorest in the classroom is among the most gifted in the class, and after reading this book you will be held responsible for finding out what your child's gift is and nurturing it. You will be held at a higher standard as far as becoming more active in your child's life. Just because your child may be academically challenged, that does not mean that they are stupid or dumb. It's just means that school is not of great interest them. So it is up to you to determine how to make school interesting to them.

Teachers!!! This is something you can also take into consideration. I only say this because I have seen teachers give up on students. This is what you signed up for! So don't cop out on the kid when the going gets tough. Be diligent in helping our young people find their talents, gifts and abilities.

Young people!!! Do not allow the harsh criticism of people to tear you down. You are gifted!!! Don't let anyone think so lowly of you that you give up on the gift God has endowed you with. If you're not doing good in school, concentrate on getting better.

Parents!! DO NOT!!! Do not kill your children's dream by planting negative comments in their heads, such as, "You will never amount to anything by practicing that stupid gift," or calling them stupid and taking away the one thing they love to do. Do not keep your child from enjoying being a kid. If they love to dance, rap, sing, write, speak, poetry, cooking, engineering, sports, or even being the next president, then you should not take that away from them with your negative comments and opinions. Just because you never amounted to anything in life doesn't mean that your kids have to end up that way. GET OVER YOURSELF!!! PAY ATTENTION TO YOUR KIDS!!!

Young people and people of all ages, please understand that there will be people who will be negative in your life, as it relates to accomplishing and walking in the gift God has so graciously blessed you with. Sadly but inevitably, some of the people who are closest to you will sometimes be the deterrent in your life. It may be a brother, sister, cousin, best friend, or even a parent who may discourage you. You have to know for yourself, without anyone confirming it for you, that this is your gift and this is what you love to do. I'm a firm believer in this statement. *When you do what you love then you will love what you do.*

As Paul states, you have to be an example or pattern for others who believe in speech, conversation, joy, love, and purity patterns. People should also be able to see the gift in you just in the manner in which you speak and in the way you conduct yourself or the way you act. This should be done in love, which means you should love what you do and love the people to whom you minister. If you absolutely do not love what you're doing, then you won't get any

138

fulfillment or joy out of doing it. If you really love what you do, you'll do it for free. It also should be done in faith or confidence. You should always be confident and sure of yourself and of God that this is what you're called to do. When you are confident about what you do, other people will be able to detect it easily.

Also, and most importantly, this should be done in purity. As I mentioned in the earlier chapters, make sure that your motives are pure when you are ministering your gift. Do not prostitute your gift. As my good friend who's also a gospel rapper told me: "The anointing is attractive," Terrance "Gifted The Flame Thrower" Veal. Many times we use our gifts for dishonest gain. Let me say that again. Often times we use our gifts in efforts to get something out of it that is not of God.

Still don't get it? Okay, well let me go deeper. Many times we use our gifts primarily to get sex, applause, standing ovations, money, and attention. We save our best for the big crowds and the so-called "celebrity status" and popularity. I must admit that being humble is probably the hardest thing to do, because most of us love to be flattered. Flattery is a very strong stimulant to the human soul. So make sure that your intentions in ministering your gift are pure and sincere.

Also, make sure that you are a person of your word. Your word is everything. Once you go back on your word, eventually it will mean nothing. When you are reliable, your word is just as good as gold. Are you reliable?

BE DEVOTED

When I looked up the word "devote," according to **Strong's Hebrew Concordance**, it means to be dedicated to something, to consecrate or to be deliberate. You have to be deliberate and purposeful in what you do. In the King James Version, it says to give attendance, which means in the Greek to be cautious or aware of; to adhere to, which means to stay attached to; to cling or cleave to. *Dictionary.com*'s version says to give up or appropriate to or concentrate on a particular pursuit, occupation, purpose, cause, etc.

What stuck out the most in this definition was the phrase, "to give up." That's a pretty significant testament to how I got to this place of doing spoken word poetry. The question is: What are you willing to give up to pursue all of what God has for you? For me, there were some things I had to give up such as lying, pleasing people, my pursuit of women, and myself. For some things to live in you, some things have got to die. I had to give up my life in the world to start my new life. It hasn't been an easy road, but God has been faithful through it all.

Are you married to God's purpose? Are you committed to service in the kingdom of God? Are you connected? We must be dedicated to the work of God, regardless of the highs and lows of ministry. Once I came to the conclusion that my gift was helping me, I became very devoted and dedicated to my work, particularly this being the work of God. I also became dedicated to doing the work of God in the aspect of ministering and performing in front of people. In doing the work of God, you must have a genuine and general care for people. You must give attendance or pay attention to the work that you do, and be careful in the way of God when doing it. In caring for the people we minister to, we must carefully exhort them, which means to encourage; to comfort; to uplift; to solace, which means to comfort in the time of sorrow or discomfort.

EXHORTATION

Exhortation is also synonymous with implore, which means to beg urgently or piteously. When we exhort, we must do with a sense of urgency. Exhortation also means to encourage; to uplift; to motivate; to invoke; to beseech; to comfort or console; to solace someone; or to entreat them. When we implore we are stressing the importance of who Christ really is. Also when we comfort, solace, or console someone, we must understand that we're not trying to tear the person down. This brings back the scripture for Proverbs when Solomon says that a soft answer turns away wrath or anger, but grievous words stir up strife (Proverbs 15:1). So we must understand that when we exhort, we should not only do it in private settings, but also in public arenas or areas.

My gift runs much deeper than poetry. However, poetry is an avenue that is utilized to exploit my gift. Exhortation is one of my gifts. I think poetry, at this stage, is one of the most quintessential arts that allow me to flow in my gift of exhortation. Many think that I'm a preacher or called be a preacher, but I will only move when God says so. Right now, poetry is where God has me. Trust me! I know how to stay in my lane. I am in no rush to preach in anybody's pulpit! LOL!!! At any rate, there should not be a place where we should not exhort, instill or teach doctrine.

Now on the other hand, there may be places where religion cannot be discussed in the public/corporate setting, such as jobs, and places of employment. However, when teaching and instilling doctrine, it does not necessarily have to be religious, especially when discussing biblical principles and doctrinal facts. Discussing principles does not mean that you are professing your faith. Biblical principles are also often used in business meetings. To quote scripture and used them to support your opinion or statement does not mean that you are preaching a sermon. It only means that you're either teaching on a certain objective or getting the person to understand your viewpoint. There will be some places where you won't be able to talk about Jesus, but your example should reflect a Christ-like lifestyle. People will see your example more than they will hear your words. When Christ is exemplified through your actions, people will be more interested in hearing what you have to say. When people become more interested in what you have to say, there won't be any reason to force your faith in others, but they will be more willing to hear you. This is why when we perform as artists, or ministering the gospel, Christ is the primary objective.

Ministry has to go forth before performance. Ministry has to go before entertainment. We have to beg urgently for the audience's attention to be focused on Christ and not be so caught up in the performance.

MINISTRY VS. ENTERTAINMENT/PERFORMANCE

Many times, we as artists get so caught in entertainment that we often times forget that we are ministers before we are artists. Well, let me speak for myself because I was there. I must admit that it is still a fight to not get so caught up in the entertainment part of the performance that we miss the ministerial part of the performance. It's hard not to straddle the fence, especially when the audience gives the energy back to the artist.

Now, I must preface this when I say that entertainment is necessary to keep the audience's attention. The scripture says in the book of Hebrews to be careful how you entertain strangers. That word means to be hospitable for the needs and the wants of guests. Also, to break it down further, "enter" means to go in; to introduce or insert; to penetrate or pierce; to present or submit. The root word "tain" means to keep up or to hold the attention of. The suffix "ment" indicates the result or the product of an action. It also indicates the mental aspect of keeping the attention of the people who give audience to you. So I don't want to undermine the importance of entertaining, because performance and entertaining are needed for the audience.

However, I also do not wish to heighten entertainment at the expense of ministry. Ministry is the primary objective, but you must also be able to perform and entertain well. If you're not able to hold the attention of the listeners, then it will be very difficult to minister in any arena, including the church! My suggestion is to work on your delivery in repetition. Take your time to articulate well and make sure that your tongue dots every I and crosses every T. Remember, this is ministry and the people you minister to have to be able to understand you clearly and coherently.

DON'T NEGLECT YOUR GIFT

Dr. King said it best, and it has been repeated by some of the greatest speakers of our time, including our current president when mentioning the famous phrase, "the fierce urgency of now." I cannot stress this enough! Please! I implore and beg you with the fiercest sense of urgency: DO NOT neglect your gift.

That word in the original Greek of the New Testament means to be careless of; to make light of; or to disregard. Other meanings are to slight something or someone; to pay little or no attention to: to be remiss in care or treatment; to omit. However, this definition speaks to me the most: to fail to carry out or perform. At one time in my life, as mentioned in previous pages, I never regarded anything I did as actually being a gift. It was something I was asked to do and I did it. I didn't treat it as a gift, neither did I recognize it as a ministry, I treated it as a task that some asked me to do. There are many of us who treat our gifts as a task and not a ministry. So as a result, we pay very little attention to it. Then there are many of us who see dollar signs with the gift, which still exudes negligence of the gift. When we are distracted by what the gift can bring, we are blinded by the true purpose of the gift.

The gift is purposed for you to give it to someone else. When people say that you are a gift to the Body of Christ, it only means that you are a tool that God chooses to use to present His gift through; that's it; nothing more, nothing less. You are only a tool being used by God. So in essence you are merely opening yourself up to be used by God as a vessel to channel His gift through you so that the Body can be exposed to the awesome omnipotence of His power. It is only His power that works through you, and you can do nothing independent of Him. Everything that you do is under the control of the Almighty and ever-living God. THANK YOU, JESUS!!!!!

Everything you do in Him is totally dependent on Him, whether you recognize it or not. When you do not acknowledge the God of the gift, that does not mean that He will take it away. The gifts come without repentance, which means God will not change His mind concerning your gift. If that were the case, I would have taken it from Lucifer. The bottom line is, when you neglect your gift you are abandoning your purpose in life.

PRACTICE YOUR GIFT

The word "practice" means to perform or do things habitually and repeatedly for the purpose of acquiring skill or proficiency. You must get in the habit of practicing and rehearsing the gift or the talent, no matter the time or the day. You must make or create the time and be committed to bettering your craft if you want to be effective in what you do. I was watching Will Smith in a YouTube clip, and he said it best: "talent you have naturally but skill can 'only' be developed from hours and hour and hours of beating up on your craft."

I have very few poems that I have written. Although I am considered a poet and a writer of poetry, I'm not really a prolific poetry writer. The few poems I have written and copyrighted are on my two albums. I have a few written from features on other people's album and some that I have not put out yet, but if I have thirty-five poems, that would be a lot for me. Some poets are prolific writers and I think that's awesome. However for me, I have to write something that's meaningful to me and it can't just be another poem. Now, I often find myself saying I don't write poems and then incorporate Jesus into the poem. But I do write God's message in the form of a poem. So if you're writing a poem or song, that's fine. However, if the song or poem doesn't have a message, then it's just another poem or song.

When you write a message, particularly God's message, whether it be in the form of poem, song, book, epistle or letter, as Paul did in the New Testament, then you can be effective in the Body of Christ. I cannot stress enough how much you have to practice. I have a habit of talking to myself, and now even answering myself. I know to some of y'all, this is crazy. Honestly, I may have just a touch of craziness in me. But this is good practice for me, because most of the time I'm not only practicing my poems but I'm also practicing what I will minister from the scripture as it relates to the poem, and elaborate on the scriptural context before I get into my poems. I also practice lecturing and doing workshops when I'm called to do so. I answer myself because I anticipate certain questions being asked of me.

So I contemplate those questions in my head and I answer them elaborately and meticulously. I want to make sure that I am specific in everything I say as it relates to kingdom work. I am often asked the question, how do I memorize all that I speak through poetry? This method of repeating the poems in my head, talking to myself constantly and practicing repetitiously, has become a habitual thing for me. It has to become a habit or like second nature to do this. I also look at interviews and talk shows like Oprah or Steve Harvey, and answer the questions they may have for the person they are interviewing. I also look at controversial talk shows like Sean Hannity and Bill O'Reilly, who interview such prolific voices as Dr. Michael Eric Dyson, who happens to be one of my inspirations in which I recite. Also I listen to Bishop T.D. Jakes, the Honorable Minister Louis Farrakhan, who's a powerful orator, and Lauryn Hill for inspiration. However, my biggest inspiration has to be without question -- aside from my grandmother -- Bishop Noel Jones. I draw inspiration from all of these powerful people and I practice as if it was going out of style. I practice by talking to and answering myself, 24/7/365.

CULTIVATE

In the midst of practicing your gift, you must also cultivate the gift. I saw a quote from a YouTube video that said, "formal education will make you a living; self education will make you a fortune." This statement doesn't mean that you should not be formally educated, because I am formally educated with a college degree. However, after being educated formally, what are you willing to do to educate yourself in the gift that God has given you? As I mentioned previously, my degree is in psychology, and I plan to further educate myself, getting my master's and doctorate degrees in a dual discipline of clinical and counseling psychology. Often times, my poems and other writing stem from the correlation between theology and psychology.

Having that in mind, cultivate means to prepare, promote or to improve the growth of a thing by labor, and attention; to develop or improve by educating and training; to train or refine. Will Smith goes on to say in his YouTube clip that, "it doesn't matter how talented you are, your talent will fail you if you're not skilled; if you don't study, work really hard, and dedicate yourself to being better every single day, you will never be able to communicate to people effectively with your artistry in the way that you want."

There goes the word "dedicated," which is synonymous to the word "devote," which was previously discussed in this book. So now then, my question to you the reader is: What steps are you taking to better yourself in your craft? People started asking, "How do you come up with your material and how do you expand your vocabulary?" I often times educate myself by reading the dictionary on a daily basis, sometimes three to four hours a day, but on average about forty-five minutes to an hour a day. I study the scripture for days at a time and for hours at a time. I want to make sure that everything that I write is based on sound biblical and doctrinal principles. My purpose is to be able to write a sermon in the form of a poem. This can only come through studying.

I also listen to preachers and sometimes the same message over and over again until it sticks, then I go to the text to study intensely for myself. Bishop Noel Jones is who I listen to for his diction and articulation and extensive knowledge of the scripture, especially from a psychological perspective. Although there are things we obviously don't agree on, I listen to Minister Farrakhan for his boldness to speak truth to power, his ability to project and command the attention of an audience, and his excellent oratorical skills. I listen to Dr. Michael Eric Dyson for his ability to defend and answer the tough questions, particularly those of controversial tones. Due to my tendency to write my poems in lyrical fashion, I listen to Lauryn Hill, not only because she sings but also because she's an excellent lyricist; one of the best ever to do it, in my opinion. Lastly I continue to educate myself on psychological issues by extensive research.

MEDITATE

As I do my extensive research, I am constantly pondering in my mind how to translate or interpret what I've learned into poems, so I jot down thoughts on paper. I'm also pondering as I type away at my laptop as we speak. Because of the fact that I have ADD, one of the symptoms of it is having ten to twenty thoughts coming into my head right behind each other, or sometimes simultaneously. Since this is what I love to do, many times I have to write down other thoughts that are coming into my head so that I won't lose my focus on the present topic, and also I won't forget about other thoughts that previously came to mind.

Although I have an attention deficit, there are things that can command and keep my attention, and this is one of them. Poetry, the dictionary, psychology, the Bible, good sound preaching and speaking all can command and keep my attention for long, extensive periods of time. So when I think of the word "meditate," it literally means to think or reflect upon something deeply; to carefully consider; to take care of; to imagine; to revolve in the mind; to consider; or something of interest. The main part of this definition is to have something of interest. My son has ADHD, but there are certain things that can command his attention for long periods of time, and he's only eight years old. Because this is my areas of interest, this is something that I can do even when I'm not trying to think about it.

Many times I wish I could turn my brain off, because it cuts into my sleep when I am resting. As a result, I'm often tired the next day at work and have to pump an unhealthy energy drink to get some kind of pick me up about myself.

When you are skilled in what you do, you are able to execute what you do effortlessly. I was watching a movie called, "Crouching Tiger, Hidden Dragon," and one of the masters of the arts says that when one is truly skilled, they will fight seemingly with no effort. Through meditation, others will be able to tell whether or not the poem that you wrote was well written and well thought out. Sometimes my poem can take anywhere from three days to three months to three years to write because of meditation.

I am often very critical of my work when I'm in meditation mode. I cannot write something that is insubstantial. If it has no significance to it, then I won't write it; I can't write it. The Bible and the dictionary are my two main tools for writing. But what good is either of them if there's not a concrete message that is tailored into these writings? It would just end up being a poem full of scriptures and big words, which may sound good to the person who may get entertained by the collaboration of big words, but won't get anything of substance out of it.

Also in verse 15 of 1 Timothy chapter 4, it says practice, cultivate, and meditate upon these duties. I must also submit that there are certain duties that come along with ministering the gift. Those duties are, as mentioned in verses 12 and 13, be an example (in the way you live) in speech, conduct, in love, in faith and purity. So whether your duty is preaching, teaching, poetry, praying for someone, or merely being a servant in the background which (v. 13) alludes to, you have to make sure that you are dedicated to the duties in which your gift shall be exploited.

THROW/GIVE YOURSELF WHOLLY

Perhaps this part of verse 15 may be the most crucial of them all. I realize over my years of school and all of the times I failed and repeated certain grades, didn't make the best grades throughout high school and college, that I really didn't give my best effort. So in essence I got out of it what I put into it. I used every excuse in the book for why I didn't make the best of grades and why I failed so many times. I used ADD as an excuse. I used the death of my grandmother as an excuse. I used Hurricane Katrina as an excuse. I would say things like "the work was too hard," or "I hate math." I used my weaknesses as a crutch, when the real truth was laziness, procrastination, doing enough to get by and not more than enough to excel.

Laziness and procrastination are a disease, and it can be contagious and contaminating. I allowed distractions to get in the way. Truthfully, I was my own distraction and used legitimate things to cover it up. My children were an excuse. "I didn't have the time to get into my gift" was also an excuse. "I work crazy long hours and that takes away from other things I want to do," "I don't have a lot of money" and "I can't afford to do this right now." "I don't have any transportation, and I don't have a job." Oh! Here's a good one! "I don't have time because my church is always depending on me to get things done!" Those were my excuses and the excuses I heard from others. All of those reasons were legitimate excuses, but nothing changes the fact that they're still just excuses, whether they're legitimate or not.

If you find something that you feel is really important, you will surely "make" the time for it. Okay, let me make it little plainer. We all "make" time for what's important. It may be understood that you don't have the time, but there are twenty-four hours in a day and most of us are not working that many hours a day. In fact, it's illegal to work that many hours a day. It is understood that your life maybe a hectic one, especially in the hustle and bustle of everyday life, but if this is important to you, you will make the effort to make it better.

That's why my testimony is so evident and indicative of this particular clause of verse 15. I went from a 1.9 GPA to a 3.7. I began to put more time and more effort into my studies and I balanced my life between school, work, and family. I didn't get as much sleep as I would've liked, but the scripture is clear when it says, "do not love sleep lest your life will end in poverty; open your eyes and you shall be satisfied with bread." (Prov. 20:13) Other scriptures say that slothfulness casts one into a deep sleep, and the idle person shall suffer hunger (Prov. 19:15).

That word "slothfulness" is just a fancy word for being lazy. In the original language it means to be indolent, which means having or showing a disposition to avoid exertion or hard work. I came to realize the reason that I did not excel at anything was not because I didn't want to work, but because I didn't want to work hard or exert myself. I wanted the work to come to me easy. I wanted to do good enough to get by. I have tried just about every short cut that one can think of, and there's just no easy way around it. You're going to have to work your butt off to get the success that you wish or desire to have.

The word "wholly" in the Greek New Testament means complete in time and amount or degree; absolute. Hmm, complete in time! Ponder on that for minute. The lack of time spent in practicing your gift will eventually spill out in your performance, especially when you're unprepared for a presentation or you're trying to cram everything in the night before. Writing this book is a manifestation of throwing yourself into the gift. My two albums "Un-Mask-U-Linity" and "Pulling Down Strongholds" and my DVD "GFSoldier Live" are also tangible manifestations of throwing myself into the gift. When you really put all of yourself into presenting your gift in exemplary fashion, your audience will see that and it will make and keep your audience more attentive, intrigued, and focused on what you have to say. There's absolutely no doubt that your audience will see the evidence or your progress when you have spent sufficient amount of time in your gift.

UNDERSTANDING THE BUSINESS OF MINISTRY

I must admit that I'm still learning in this area, but I'm growing to understand it every single day. I now understand that people in the church will use you up just as much as the world would use you up. The only difference is, the church will use you up and call it God. At least the world will deceive some other kind of way. So I had to understand at the time when I was broke, rebuilding from Hurricane Katrina, and re-locating to Texas that I needed gas in my car to move around in Dallas. Dallas is a whole lot bigger than New Orleans and it takes longer to get around. There were times when people didn't want to put gas in my tank. People would promise me money for gas and I would make it to the event with an empty tank of gas, with no way of getting back home.

Then I realized that I had to start taking this ministry more seriously. People will only take you as seriously as you take yourself and your ministry. So I had to start making requests for compensation, especially if I wanted to provide for my family. Now don't get me wrong, I still do free events when I can afford to do them. There will be times when people will offer compensation. There will also be times when people will ask what you charge. I never thought that it would get to this point, but it did. I was always one to say, "However God leads you." And that's okay, but you should be more discerning in determining who to say that to. I know that it's very difficult to request compensation from people. Believe me, it's still a struggle for me because I don't want to run the people off. However, even in making requests there will be times when people will "mistakenly" forget to compensate you. This has happened to me so many times. There will also be times when people will say they will compensate you and have no intentions of doing it at all.

Eventually I had to start drawing up formal documented agreements to get compensated because too many people were getting the best of me. Let's not get this misconstrued, people. Part of ministry growth as it relates to expansion will take some kind of funding and financial support, especially when you're trying to make music, an album or CD, write a book, or travel expenses. You won't be able to do this on selling your product alone, which is also a quick lesson I had to learn. I went to an event in Chicago last year and ministered to a packed house of over 1,500 people. With the power and the anointing of the Holy Spirit, I brought the house down! Killed it!!!! I only sold six CDs. Did you hear me? SIX!!!! Although I was disappointed with the sales, I still had a great time hanging out with some of my fellow poets! Just because there's a huge crowd on hand to witness your craft or artistry, that doesn't mean you will make great product sales. Many times I've been in a room of 75-100 people and walked away with $400 in product sales. So you can't always be so sure that your product will sell just because the crowd is big.

Make sure that you are very thorough in your agreement forms and specific about your desires. The more professional you are, the more professional your patrons will be. As mentioned before, there some events that I will continue to do for free, but as your presence becomes more of a demand, you must consider being compensated. There are times when I have to take off from work to make it to an event. You have to be compensated for your time away from work, school, family, etc. I can't take off from work to do a free event when I have to keep the lights on and food on the table. Get my drift? Your patronage can come in abundance, but you have to dedicate yourself to becoming better every day and in every aspect of your ministry, including the business side of it.

Once again, this is what I've learned so far from other friends of the craft who have passed their knowledge on to me. Don't ever be afraid to ask questions of someone who may be more knowledgeable than you are on a particular topic as it relates to your ministerial artistry. I ask questions all the time. Remember, you have to remain a good student of your craft in every area. Truthfully, when people see your progression as an artist, more than likely they'll be willing to offer compensation and they will definitely inquire about the monetary aspect of your ministry.

YOUR PROGRESS MAY BE EVIDENT

I'll be the first to say that I love what I do, and I truly believe that when one really loves what he or she does, they will do it for free. I know for sure that if I never make another dollar from doing this, I'll still be writing, speaking and exhorting. People will definitely see your progress. By the grace of God I have traveled nationally and internationally due to the progress that this has brought. God will definitely allow the gift to make room for you and bring you before great people if He sees that you are serious about your gift (Proverbs 18:16). That word "progress" means a movement toward a goal or to further or higher stage; growth or development. To go deeper with the word "progress," it is translated as "profiting" in the King James Version. "Profiting" in the Greek translation of New Testament King James text means advancement; increase, furtherance, or gain.

Now let me get a little deeper. Your progress may or may not come in monetary or superficial value. What I mean by that is your success is based on your growth and maturity. Remember, your conduct must also be an open manifestation and an example of who God is through your gift. How you conduct yourself is the first order of business as it relates to your growth or advancement. If you cannot conduct yourself in a godly manner, then surely you're not suited to minister to the masses. When I say the masses, I could mean only one person, who may run and tell others about the goodness of your gift or the lack thereof because of a poor attitude. Your conduct will ultimately determine how others will receive you, regardless of how skilled you are. If you have no discipline, no humility, no integrity, faith, or love, and faith is mentioned in verse 12, then you can be assured that you won't be received in that sentiment.

Love and faith are also called fruits of the Spirit, as Paul also talks about in Galatians chapter 5. Other fruits of the Spirit include temperance (self-control), gentleness (kindness), goodness (integrity), joy (gladness), which are other areas of conduct that you will have to practice in the maturation process. Skill won't mean anything if you have a jacked up personality. So I make sure that I'm clear on this as it relates to your progress, because your progress has to be made evident in every area of your ministry, and good conduct, by far, has to be the most important part of it.

Now on other hand, I can't say that you won't make money from what you do, especially when you have a passion and love for it. What I can say is that God rewards those who diligently seek Him. I also want to add that if you don't see the increase, gain, or advancement in the financial side of this, that does not mean that your success is not coming in other areas of your ministry. So if you quit because the money is not quite coming in, it only means that you were in it for all of the wrong reasons. The scripture says, "What shall a man profit if he gains the world and lose his soul?" The world is not just limited to money. There's also fame, popularity, attention, cars, and houses. So if you're doing this for any of these reasons, then you're absolutely not fit to spread the gospel of Jesus Christ. Although you are in the world, you're not of it. You're not supposed to get into ministry to see what you can get out of it. You get into this for what God can get out it! Although there's money that can be made from what you do, if you're only in it for money and self-seeking gratification, you might as well quit right now. God does not operate in that manner. Your personality has to be able to reflect what God has made evident in your life.

LOOK WELL TO YOURSELF [TO YOUR OWN PERSONALITY]

I really needed to meditate and ponder on this clause of verse 16 before I wrote this particular paragraph. In the King James Version, it says to take heed to thyself, which means pay attention to yourself. Make sure that your presentation is one that will be acceptable by all who are drawn to your ministry/artistry. Make sure that you are dressed appropriately for the occasion. You have to be able to make an impression on the people to whom you are presenting the gospel. Also, when you are presenting your craft, the scripture says minister according to your own personality.

Now, I may not have translated this correctly, but here is how I interpret "to your own personality" in my own exegetical imagination. If you are an impostor or a person who plagiarizes, STOP IT!! To plagiarize is to copy or take someone else's work and present it as if it's your own work. Living in this modern era of the hip hop generation, we call this biting. When someone bites another person's rhymes or lines, it is considered stealing someone else's work. So I strongly encourage the writer, poet, author, or artist to copyright ALL of your work. This can be done online by the United States Copyright Office, or you can go to the Library of Congress website and click on copyright.

I have a good buddy who successfully put out an album that I have today. There were two poems that I particularly remember from listening to his CD. Well, one day I went to an open mic night and I heard one of his poems. I knew that I heard that poem before, but for some reason it didn't register with me at the time. However, the following month I went back and saw the same guy and he did another poem from my buddy's album. Then it hit me. I knew who those poems belonged to. So I confronted the guy about it and never saw him at another open mic again. I asked him, did he write those poems, and he told me yes. However, the popular website for artists at the time was Myspace. I told him that I knew a guy who had an album out and those poems were uploaded to Myspace. Also I told other people about it, including a guy who had a laptop and wifi to be able go to Myspace. The guy who recited the poems came up with some lame excuse why he had to leave, but he knew he was busted.

At any rate, make sure you do your own work according to your own personality and be true to what you teach.

TAKE HEED TO YOUR TEACHINGS

One of the things that frustrates me about this particular verse is when teachers of the gospel teach that which they have not conquered on their own. In the book of James, he gives very sound advice for people who have ambitions to teach the gospel. Let's see what James has to say about people who are so exuberant to be teachers of the gospel.

James 3

Amplified Bible (AMP)

3 Not many [of you] should become teachers ([a]self-constituted censors and reprovers of others), my brethren, for you know that we [teachers] will be judged by a higher standard and with greater severity [than other people; thus we assume the greater accountability and the more condemnation].

2 For we all often stumble and fall and offend in many things. And if anyone does not offend in speech [never says the wrong things], he is a fully developed character and a perfect man, able to control his whole body and to curb his entire nature.

When we teach, there should be something about us that indicates not only have we studied this Word, but we have also experienced it. Many of us do a very good job of studying the text for the purpose of good homiletic presentation and pulpit oratory. However due to the lack of experience in a certain area, it's not as effective because there's no story or testimony to back up the teaching. That's one of the many reasons I purposely wrote this book. This is not only for the purpose of giving information, but to give a substratum of testimony to validate the information given. Your testimony is by far the best sermon anyone can preach or teach, in my opinion. What good are we as artists, preachers, and teachers of the gospel to the Body of Christ if we've never been through anything and lived to tell it? How can we preach deliverance if we've never been delivered?

I truly believe that good teachings come from good testimonies. If you have no testimonies in which to preach, teach, recite from, then your teachings can still be good but will lack power. Remember, the scripture says that people overcame the accuser not only by the blood of the Lamb, but also by the word or utterance of their testimony (Revelation 12:10-12). So the more you study and meditate in the gift, the more you will develop the capacity to teach with conviction, transparency, and testimony.

Teaching is also one of my gifts, and most of the poetry I write is teaching-oriented. However, I consider myself a student, not a teacher. I am a student of many. I am a student of the text (Bible). I'm a student of many who have inspired me to do what I do. I am a student of my grandmother. I am student of my pastor. I am a student of my children. I am a student of other poets. I am a student of good preaching and preachers who teach well. Most of my inspiration comes from gleaning from good preachers, which I've mentioned already. I'm always readily available to learn from something or someone. Continuing to be a student and learning from others is probably my strongest suit, even though I am still lazy at times. I truly believe that for someone to become a good teacher, they must first be a good student and always be willing to learn and be taught. Being a student is an ever-growing and ongoing process. The best teacher is simply the best student of learning. You must be apt at learning to be a good teacher.

With that being said, my other gift is knowledge, and I truly believe that is how this gift was and still is being developed. Knowledge is also mentioned by Paul as one of the gifts of the Spirit (1 Corinthians 12:8) I like how the Amplified Bible puts it.

1 Corinthians 12:8

Amplified Bible (AMP)

[8] To one is given in and through the [Holy] Spirit [the power to speak] a message of wisdom, and to another [the power to express] a word of knowledge and understanding according to the same [Holy] Spirit;

This is how all of the gifts that God has given me flow in unison with each other. To speak and express are both coupled with the gift of exhortation, especially when it is a message of wisdom and a word of knowledge. I have a deep passion for knowledge and I am always excited to let people know what I've learned.

What are your gifts? What passion do you have that burns inside of you right now? What are you waiting on? Start today and watch how God will expand your territory as it relates to walking in your gift. Now, there may be some tough times as it relates to walking in your gift, but that should not stop if you are persistent in your walk. Your trials are there to help strengthen you as you grow in your gift.

PERSEVERE IN THESE THINGS

Perseverance is probably one of the most difficult qualities that one has to possess to develop the character of the person who is a recipient of the gift. Character is never easily developed! It unequivocally developed through a series of tests and trials. There is absolutely NO way around it. James says it best.

James 1:2-4

Amplified Bible (AMP)

² Consider it wholly joyful, my brethren, whenever you are enveloped in or encounter trials of any sort or fall into various temptations.

³ Be assured and understand that the trial and proving of your faith bring out endurance and steadfastness and patience.

⁴ But let endurance and steadfastness and patience have full play and do a thorough work, so that you may be [people] perfectly and fully developed [with no defects], lacking in nothing.

When I look at the word "perseverance," I see other synonyms that are interdependent of it, such as endurance and patience. Perseverance lets me know that there will be some very uncomfortable times ahead of me. The question that perseverance asks is: Will I quit if something doesn't go right or will I continue to walk in my gift in spite of the trials I will endure? Jesus says it is impossible for you to not suffer affliction, but woe unto the man through whom the affliction comes (Luke 17:1). So please understand, there is absolutely nothing you can do to avoid the affliction. The question is: What are you going to do when the affliction comes? Will you fold and buckle under the pressure, or will you continue to push through? Solomon says that your strength is small if you fail in the time of adversity (Proverbs 24:10).

Tests and trials will come, especially when you are anointed and gifted. So get ready! It is through the testimony of your trials and tribulations and God bringing you out that makes your message (poems, songs, sermons, etc.) more powerful. Many people want the success but don't want to go through anything to get the success. Perseverance is one of the major prerequisites in accomplishing our goals. If you have no stamina, endurance, or steadfastness, then how can you possibly handle the hardships that come along with success if you won't through the necessary obstacles to get there? As long as you're walking in your gift, it should give you some kind of comfort and peace in knowing that trials are only tests to strengthen you. Your gifts should be therapeutic when you exercise them correctly in the way God would have for you to do. I must also mention that prayer has to be a part of this persevering process.

PRAY IN YOUR PERSEVERANCE.

I must admit at this very moment that this was a very flaky process for me. I really did not understand what a relationship with God really meant. I assumed that everyone who was gifted by God and practiced their gifts skillfully had a relationship with God. I think many people assume that there's a relationship with God when they see people minister in such an effective way.

That is the furthest thing from the truth. I will say this again. Your anointing does not dispel your humanity. (Q27) Just because you are anointed to do what you do, it doesn't mean that you're in a right relationship with God. It doesn't mean that you have a prayer life, either. I've been doing poetry for a while. I've been ministering studying, and learning the scripture for quite a while. The result of my study was made evident before the people who listen to me, and the people were blessed when they heard it. But as I have said before, just because God uses you doesn't mean that He approves of you. He uses the foolish things of this world to confound or confuse you. Just because He used you doesn't mean that He knew you!!! I know this may sound redundant, so please excuse me. But you need to hear this, especially from someone who really didn't care to take time out to pray. Yes! I'm talking about me!

If you really go to God with a heart of contrition and brokenness, HE HEARS YOU!!!! I am a living witness: GOD HEARS YOU!!! He also will respond to you at the appropriate time and will use the most unlikely avenue to manifest His response to your prayer. When I hear the passage that says He uses the foolish things of the world to confound the wise, it tells me that He will do it in the most

169

unlikely way. So you absolutely cannot omit or ignore any avenues in which God will speak. He speaks through children, alcoholics, drug addicts who may be under the influence, pimps, prostitutes, liars, animals, etc. God will use anyone or anything to communicate His message. Nothing is off limits for God as it relates to how He communicates with you.

I witnessed this for myself just recently. I was at the end of my rope with temptation. I just couldn't take it anymore. I said to Him, "You have to do or say something because I have no more strength to resist this." He spoke to me the next morning at 5am on 05/22/2013 through a radio show. He will not always use your pastor to speak a word to you. So you cannot have limits to who will speak a word to you. Many times we're quick to disqualify certain people because of their lack of scriptural knowledge, education, or church experience. Many times, wisdom can also come from the people who you have disqualified or have written off as being an able witness. There's more hope for a fool than a man who is wise in his own conceit. Don't become the one who is wise in his own mind, because even a fool can have a word from God. Make yourself susceptible to all avenues of communication. God is the knower of all things; the omniscient One. He can use the very evil that's going on in and around you to speak a word of truth. HE'S GOD!! LOL!! HELLOOO!!! C'mon now!!

For this section, I admonish you, implore you, urgently beg you, and desperately plead with you to make this your daily practice. Prayer is a very crucial necessity and an integral component/weapon of warfare to utilize in this persevering process. Paul says to the Roman church that you must be patient in tribulation but continue constantly and instantly in prayer (Romans 12:12).

Prayer has to be the substratum of everything you do as it pertains to the gift and life in general. Prayer has to be the foundation in which you minister in your calling. God still has to have His time. (Q28) You cannot be so caught up in the ministry of God that you forget to minister to God. You cannot get so caught in the external intricacies of God that you miss or neglect the internal intimacy of God. Make sure not to get so caught up in practical outward adorning tendencies, that you miss the spiritual inward propensities. (Q29) God has to be first in all that you do in ministry. Many times we equate doing the ministry of God or doing God's work with doing God's will. Just because you're doing God's work, it doesn't necessarily mean you're doing His will. This is why prayer is necessary and a requirement, because there may be some work that He doesn't want you to do. Not all work is good work, and just because you're doing it in the name of Jesus doesn't necessarily mean that Jesus is in it.

Okay, let me put it another way. You should be careful of saying yes to every phone call or email you get concerning your gift, because God won't always be at the forefront of every phone call or email you get. Not every event that has God's name on it is godly. As the scripture says in the gospel according to Mark, these people make a big show of saying all of the right things, but their heart is not in it. "They act like they are worshipping me but they really don't mean it. They just use me as a cover up to preach whatever suits their fancy" (Mark 7:5-9 Mess). This is why time spent with God is a must. You have to be careful not spend so much time *doing* the work of God that it takes away from your time spent *with* Him. So I say this with urgency: You have to pray!! Amen? You also have to be able to prioritize correctly.

THE ANOINTING VS. RELATIONSHIP

Let me start this section by keeping this plain and simple. Your anointing has nothing to do with your relationship with God. Although the anointing is attractive, as my good friend, Terrence "Gifted the FlameThrowa" Veal would say, it does not dispel your humanity. I know that many will disagree with this statement, and that's okay. I'm only speaking of my experiences of being in the anointing and still pounding my chest because I got the standing ovation I wanted.

I will say this once again. Your anointing does not dispel your humanity. Let's walk through this. When I wrote my two albums, those poems were a result of hard work, many hours of studying, and constantly working on my skill set. Although God is still the facilitator of those duties, that has nothing to do with spending time in prayer with Him. Anyone can develop a skill if they spend a sufficient amount of time in doing it. Once you have the gift, God does not take that away from you. What you decide to do with your gift is up to you. However, whether you do for God or do for the world in the name of God, your skill concerning the gift is no different from the one who uses their gift for worldly gain if you don't spend time at His feet.

One of my more famous poems, "Exegesis of Jesus," was a direct result of biblical studies, which is a definite necessity. I spent enough time in the text to pull that poem out of the Bible. When I performed that piece for a well-known world-wide ministry in Los Angeles, the anointing did flow quite heavily when I performed it. The people and ministry were blessed. However, on the inside I was caught up in pride, ego, and flattery because of the loud cheers, the compliments, and particularly the recognition. It was the world-wide recognition that I would receive that would ultimately shift my focus away from God.

Unfortunately, there's an exponential increase of people in the body of Christ who are becoming more focused on becoming famous than doing the will of God. Some of us would rather see our name in the headlines or billboards than to see our name in the Lamb's book of life. VERY DANGEROUS!

Another poem that I performed in Chicago for a ministry that is also an up-and-coming, well-known ministry was also a result of studying the Word and spending time with practicing the skill. The results were the same. The anointing flowed heavily, but I was still caught up in pride. Please understand, the Spirit of God will flow in the gift because there are lives at stake, lost souls that need to be saved, and people who need to be inspired. However, that doesn't mean that the Spirit lives in you just because the anointing of the Spirit flows through you.

Let me put it another way: just because the anointing is on you doesn't necessarily constitute the Spirit dwelling within you! I need you to really take heed to what I am about to say. Please be careful not to walk around doing the work of God with the spirit of Lucifer!!!

THE SPIRIT OF LUCIFER

Yeah! I'm going there! This is where I was. I was walking around, very busy doing the works of God, but had my own selfish intentions. I was very busy in the community inspiring people, teaching people young and old, had people who looked up to me, and asking me to mentor them. Now don't get me wrong. I gave them the absolute truth based on my knowledge, experience, wisdom, and sound biblical principles/doctrine. But that still doesn't put you in relationship with God. I don't mean to sound redundant but I have to get this into your system so there won't be any excuse going forward. As I said in the previous chapters, telling the truth is not the same as being truthful.

I was teaching and ministering the word and the works of God with the spirit of Lucifer. Let us explore the story of Lucifer for those of us who are not familiar with this story. Lucifer was one of God's most prestigious, intellectually and artistically gifted angels in heaven. He was basically God's right-hand man. Lucifer was also exceptionally gifted in the artistic expression and may have been one of the more pleasurable angels to look upon. The other angels in heaven also looked up to him. He was awe-inspiring, and many of heaven's angels absolutely adored him.

However, Lucifer also had a deeply rooted issue with pride. He also took credit for the works that he had done. He allowed the gift to shift his focus away from God. He did the work of God and flowed heavily in the ministry of God. He became so skilled and good at what he did that he became arrogant in the gift that only one person could have given to him. God! He was cast into hell, not so much for something he verbalized, but for the pride he had in his heart. He boasted so much pride inside that his heart spoke more arrogance than he could have ever said with his mouth. Let's observe the scripture:

Isaiah 14:12-15

Amplified Bible (AMP)

[12] How have you fallen from heaven, O [a]light-bringer and daystar, son of the morning! How you have been cut down to the ground, you who weakened and laid low the nations [O blasphemous, satanic king of Babylon!]

[13] And you said in your heart, I will ascend to heaven; I will exalt my throne above the stars of God; I will sit upon the mount of assembly in the uttermost north.

[14] I will ascend above the heights of the clouds; I will make myself like the Most High.

[15] Yet you shall be brought down to Sheol (Hades), to the innermost recesses of the pit (the region of the dead).

The traditional King James actually mentions the name Lucifer. When breaking down the etymology of the word, it literally means "the bringer of dawn." Some translations suggest that Lucifer means "shining one." He was doing the works of God but his heart was not in the will of God. His was recognized as one of the prominent entities in heaven. However, when he tried to make himself to be like God and the boss of his ministry, that's what orchestrated his sudden descent into the place of death, or hell as some scholars would translate.

I want to make sure that we as artists and ministers of the gospel understand the danger in wanting to be the next star, the next big name, the next celebrity, or the next one to shine. Having this mentality takes the focus off of God, and now the focus is on the recipient of the gift more than the Giver of the gift. This is very dangerous territory. It took me quite some time to realize what I was doing. I knew that eventually I had to get my act together.

That's the reason why this book was written. It is written as an urgent warning to all who will hear or read. It's okay to be the best that God wants you to be, the fame may come, and you may even achieve celebrity status. But when that becomes your main focus and it becomes all about being better than the next person for the mere purpose of getting your shine on, that's when the danger starts.

WHEN MINISTRY BECOMES COMPETITION

As I've mentioned in the beginning, some of these things are very difficult to talk about. Competition is not a bad thing. It becomes bad when it is the main focus that drives you. Competition is a natural thing that we do as human beings, believe it or not. We compete to win a prize. We compete for recognition. We compete for promotion. We compete to gain the interest of a company, job, woman or man, and there's nothing wrong with that. Competition is an innate entity that dwells in us and drives us to become better.

Here's my issue with ministry. I believe competition becomes a bad thing when it takes away one's capacity to be sensitive, considerate, and sincere towards people. It becomes a bad thing when you're the only one that wants the spotlight. I think competition is bad when it distracts you from the people whom we minister to. When competition for membership becomes more important than winning souls, it's a problem. As a result, we have an 80,000-member church and only 1,000 of them are actually saved; when entertainment supersedes ministry. There's a fine line in ministry when competition starts to become the forefront of all your ministry engagement. This is one of my current struggles. The only reason I have this under control is because I am able to confess these things before God. In turn, God gives me the strength to overcome these struggles.

One of the things I've learned about God is that He doesn't necessarily take the pain away or get rid of the struggle. But He gives us the strength to overcome or deal with it. As long as I am real with myself and to God, I can overcome anything. So can you! I now realize that had it not been for these struggles, I would not be able to talk or write about them. I wouldn't be able to minister to people effectively if I cannot deal with these struggles in my own life. God allows these struggles to remain prevalent in my life so that I can be totally dependent on Him for my strength. Jesus mentioned to Paul that His grace is sufficient, that His strength is made perfect in our weaknesses. If we're trying to be strong on our own, then there's no room for Him to perfect His strength in us. So as I confess my weaknesses He's making me strong.

But you must become strong enough be weak so that He can make you strong in Him. WOW!! Hold Up! YOU MUST BECOME STRONG ENOUGH TO BE WEAK!!! You must become strong enough to let these things go. And once you have used up your strength to let these things go, He will replenish that strength abundantly. It's extremely hard to let go and it takes a great deal of strength to be subject to that kind of weakness. But this is what I believe we must do to be successful in overcoming our struggles. Our true competition should be for winning souls to Christ. Satan, of course, is our fierce competitor.

FOR THE MARRIED FOLK

To be married and manage ministry can be a very difficult thing to manage. One of the biggest misconceptions about being married and having a ministry is thinking that success in ministry means success in marriage. That concept is the furthest from the truth. It's actually the other way around. Success in marriage has to be at the forefront of having a good ministry. Just because your ministry may appear to be successful doesn't mean that you are successful in God. Remember, success in God doesn't always come in monetary or superficial value, especially when it comes to God. Money, cars, clothing, houses, big sanctuaries, fame, popularity are mere physical and tangible manifestations of being successful in ministry. Love, joy, peace, longsuffering, humility, gentleness, temperance, faith, and goodness are all spiritual and intangible manifestations of God. And I truly believe that the only way can you reach a pinnacle of success in God is to conquer these characteristics of the spirit.

Having the appearance of being successful is not the same as being successful. Consciously, many people put so much into ministry and purposely neglect their homes. Sadly, many spitefully use ministry and the works of God as an excuse to justify their marital impotence. This is not pleasing to God. The scripture is very clear that if many can't take care of business or manage in their own home, then how can they be equipped to handle or manage the business of God (1 Timothy 3:5)? Make sure that you prioritize and not put your ministry before your marriage, because that's also displeasing to God.

You must understand that marriage is your first ministry. Marriage is the first ministry/institution created by God when He created man, and you must honor your husband/wife.

SPOUSE VS. HUSBAND/WIFE

One day I was talking to a friend of mine and we were on the topic of marriage. He felt as if he was justified in cheating because of what he wasn't getting at home. He was faithful to his wife and still is. However, there was a period of intense struggle as it relates to their marriage. Eventually I began talking them both and she didn't see anything wrong with her negligence in that area. So it was hard to convince her otherwise. I felt privileged that both would come to me, but it was obvious they needed more help than I could give them. But I did notice something there in both of them. I noticed that they were married, but didn't have a marriage.

Today we have very unhappy couples at the expense of marriage. There are many people who are married but don't have a marriage. So please understand, being married doesn't always constitute marriage. So I began to understand that although they were espoused to each other, they had yet to become husband and wife. They asked what was the difference. I simply said that when you signed that legal document, you signed in a space where it says spouse's signature. This only means that on paper, you are legally or lawfully married by whichever state you live in. Just because you're that person's spouse, it doesn't mean that you're their husband or wife. Spouse only means that you are married.

Wife or husband means that you have a marriage. Being a spouse is just a mere title. Being a husband or wife is a ministry. Many people want the title but don't want the ministry that comes along with the title. Many people want to be married, but don't want the marriage. If you are married, then marriage becomes your first ministry. If you're not willing to die to yourself and give up yourself for the sake of marriage, then it's best that you stay single in an effort to avoid divorce. It is better to say no than it is to say yes.

Here's a great example: If you have a relationship with God, then you're not only married to Him, but you have a marriage with Him. However, if you are in a backslidden stage of your life where you fall out of relationship with Him, then He still stays married to you regardless of your sin. He just wants you to return to Him and repent. This is what's happening in other forms of ministry today. Many people in the church want the title, but are not willing to take on the responsibility it takes to wear that title. Some of us just want to perform and become a star or celebrity, but don't want to take the time out to pray or minister to someone who needs prayer. This is also another form of backsliding, in my opinion.

We have ignored the things of God and have prostituted ourselves for fame, popularity, and performance. If you can't say Amen, it's okay to say "ouch." Don't worry, I have said "ouch" to this on many occasions!

SAVING YOURSELF AND THOSE WHO HEAR YOU

This is probably my most favorite part of the whole book to write about. I am a living testimony of how this gift has saved my life. In the Greek translation of the King James New Testament, that word "save" means to heal. If your gift does not save/heal you first, then your gift is not saving anyone who listens to you. If your gift does not minister to you first and effectively, then how can you effectively minister to the ones who hear you? If your gift does absolutely nothing but make you a few dollars and make you popular, what effect are you really having in the body? These are questions that you must ask yourself before you minister in your craft.

Are you following the proper guidelines as it relates to scripture when you're ministering the gift? I will say this again: your testimony as it relates to the gift is probably the most powerful tool one can use in ministering your gift. The people have to be able to see the progress, the growth, and transformation in you; not just in monetary or superficial gain, because they may never happen. This gift is my catharsis, which means an emotional cleansing or purging of the soul, especially through certain types of artistic expression. In psychology it is said that catharsis is a technique used in psychology that is utilized to relieve tension and anxiety by bringing repressed feelings and fears to consciousness. Spoken word poetry just happens to be my artistic choice of emotional release, which keeps me from holding on to suppressed and repressed feelings.

There's definitely healing in what we do as artists and as gifted people of God. Healing is also one of the spiritual gifts mentioned by Paul in 1 Corinthians. If the gift is properly handled in the way the Paul instructs us, and if we are able to save/heal ourselves and those who hear us, it appears that the gift of healing has also been developed in us. For example, this reminds me of the story of David, who was skilled in playing a harp. David was said to be a man of war, a valiant man, prudent in speech and eloquent, an attractive man with beautiful eyes and fine looking, who played the harp skillfully, and the Lord was with him (1 Samuel 16:12,18). When the Spirit of the Lord departed from Saul, there was another spirit that came upon him that the Bible calls an evil spirit of the Lord. This spirit is interpreted as one that torments. So Saul was tormented or troubled, and he acquired David because his servants told him of his skill to play the harp. When David arrived at Saul's palace, he served him and ministered to him and it pleased Saul so much that he kept David as one of his servants. When the evil spirit of the Lord came upon Saul, David played the harp and Saul became well and the evil spirit left him (1 Samuel 16:23). Saul only became well or healed when David skillfully played his harp. This was one of David's artistic expressions of playing music.

David was also a masterful poet, as he wrote many poems [quibble: some of the Psalms have other people's names on them, for instance, Moses wrote one of them, and the sons of Korah wrote some -- so if there are 150 Psalms total, David didn't write every Psalm. <G>] in the book of Psalms. However, the sons of Korah wrote in Psalm 45, says that the heart or emotions were overflowing with a good theme. It goes on to say that they speak of things which he has made touching the king and their tongue is the pen of a ready writer. The New Living Translation says that beautiful words stir my heart, my tongue is the pen of a skillful poet (Psalm 45:1). David is clearly expressing himself about what his gift does for him. His gift stirs his heart.

At first it was hard to give specifics on how the gift saved my life. I would always say that God was who saved my life. However, since we know that God is a God who saves lives, that explanation tends to be a bit broad and generalized. Although God is the ultimate reason why my life was saved and healed at the time, there had to be some steps taken in that healing process. I had to be more detailed to the people I ministered to, to be effective. God will always give you information as it relates to bringing you out of a situation, and it is your duty to meditate, practice, and study that information. You must be diligent in what you do and be willing to work hard and not be a lover of sleep. I understand that you will need some rest. However, you should only get the rest that is needed to be able to function well. This is how I have evolved and grown as a human being, let alone a man of God. There's no way to avoid the growing pains of God's purpose.

CONCLUSION

This book is a comprehensive look at how the gift has saved my life and how it can ultimately save yours. Although you may experience different situations, trials, and circumstances, there's still no way around this process. The principles that I have shared are concrete biblical principles, based on my testimony. If there was another way to do it, I would've probably done it by now. This gift has allowed me to go places that I would not have dreamed of. Although I have had visions of going places, I didn't think it would come as soon as it did. I was out of the country before I actually was able to get to New York or Florida. I was expecting to travel the nation before I traveled abroad. But God saw fit to do otherwise. What a mighty and on time God we serve!!

I pray that this book helps you, the reader, to understand this process, as I am still learning this process as I go along. I'm not where I wish to be, but I do understand that this is a process and I don't want to be where I shouldn't be before it is my time to be there. Catch my drift? Many times we want so badly to be in a place of success in our lives even when we're not ready to handle that type of success. I can only speak for myself. I know that there's a certain place in success that I am totally not ready for because there are certain parts of my flesh that I'm still dealing with. I'm a man, so I am still dealing with this incredibly large ego of mine. Pride goes before the fall or destruction, and I don't want to destroy myself by moving away from the path that God has me on.

So as Solomon says, I want to be able to trust the Lord with all my heart and lean not to my own understanding, but give reference to Him in all of my ways and doings that He can navigate my road to success in Him, not in the world. I pray that this book has ministered to you ans had led you back to God and communion with Him. I hope and pray that you can once again establish an intimacy with Him that you once may have lost with Him.

This book is not a "how to" kind of book. Sometimes I'm leery of those types of books. But this is a "how I," because you may have a different way of getting there. On the other hand, there are critical principles in the book that must be practiced faithfully, or you won't reach or accomplish your goals, dreams, or ambitions. If you've heard the principles being preached before and they have become a nuisance to you, then it's probably an indication that you should take heed to these principles. I know you may be tired of hearing the same things over and over again. Trust me, I can also attest to that.

I always used to think that it can't be that simple. I must say to you that it really is that simple. It may not be that easy. But it is that simple. There's a huge difference between something being easy and simple. Something may be simple to figure out, but may be hard to do. What I mean by that is although it may be simple, it may take an all-out effort to accomplish it. To get a degree, you will have to go to school, middle school, high school, and college to get there. The plan seems simple, but it takes hard work to execute the plan.

We serve a God of simplicity, not complexity. God gives us simple or basic instructions, but He never said the process of His simplicity is easy. Every simple task has a process. Now, the process may become easier to do because you have spent an extensive amount of time perfecting it. When you have spent numerous quality hours in doing this particular task, eventually it becomes a skill to do and it comes to you easily. But it wasn't always that easy in the beginning. Walking is very simple and it may be easy for the person aged four and above. However, for the newborn or a baby who is about eight to ten months old, the process will be hard for them, although it may be simple. However, by the time they get to age four, it will have become very easy for them. A person who has gotten into an accident and is learning to walk again will have to work hard to get back to their regular form of walking.

We should not despise or take for granted the simple things in life, because God uses the foolish or simple things of this world to confound the wise.

THE FOOLISHNESS OF GOD (1 COR. 19-29)

I know there are times in life when things don't sound right. Since the brain of the human being is a complex organism, we are often analytical. Many times we tend to complicate what God has made so simple. We over-analyze, we look too deep into certain situations and circumstances. We often hear God, but very seldom do we listen to Him. We tend to complicate matters, because in a sense we try to have things all figured out when it comes to God. We tend to be very critical of His tactics. So when we educate ourselves, we think we are at a place where we have Him figured out. However, being that our thoughts are not His thoughts and our ways are not His ways, we need to understand that we are not going have everything figured out.

We tend to worry when we don't have everything figured out. In turn, we let doubt set in, which stems from extensive worrying. One of the reasons why we get to a place of worry and doubt is because we think we know everything instantly. We want to know what's going to take place in the future right now. We don't want to wait. We don't want to be patient. Some of us really want to be God. We want to know everything. However we don't have the capacity to be able to handle this world if we knew everything. Many times we tend to think that God doesn't make sense. Sometimes He doesn't make any sense, in my opinion. But that's what makes Him God. There will be times when He doesn't make any sense because He's not human. He's not supposed to make human sense. He's supposed to make godly sense. I'm shouting that!!!

And godly sense doesn't have to make human sense because as humans we are not always godly!! Talk back to me!! He gives the kind of peace that surpasses all human intellect, knowledge, wisdom, and understanding. Look at what the scripture says about this. It says that the "foolishness of God is wiser than men." It doesn't matter how smart you are or how many degrees you have, there's absolutely nothing you can do to figure Him out. He uses what we think is foolish and puts our knowledge to shame. So I encourage you to wait until God reveals it to you, because you will surely stress yourself trying to figure it out on your own.

We have to have faith that God will be God. We know that without faith it is impossible to please Him. We must begin to establish a faith that is unwavering. Just because it has not been revealed to you doesn't mean that God is not on His job. No one can do it better. LOL!! We have a difficult enough job being humans, and we have the nerve to try to tell God how to do His job. So let's be clear: God doesn't make sense!! So we have to wait for God to make it make sense for us and stop trying to figure Him out.

STILL TRIFLING?

Perhaps! Maybe so…I would say a categorical yes. I still entertain those trifling thoughts because this is what I struggle with on a daily basis. That is why it is imperative that we die daily. John specifically states "all that is in the world, the lust of the flesh, the lust of the eyes, and the pride of life." This is a very powerful scripture. This reminds me that when I walk out of my door, the temptation is there. My eyes will be open and I will be observant of my struggles. I will like what I see, but I have to exhibit the power that God gives me to flee and not give in to it. Yes, I am trifling. But I have learned how to exercise the spirit of self-control. Yes, I'm still a ho [the slang for whore is ho, if that's what you prefer to use. <G> LOL!! I'm well aware of that, thanks for bringing that to my attention] in my desires and in my thoughts. But I die to those thoughts daily. There's not a day that goes by that these thoughts don't cross my mind. But repentance and contrition are a must, and are a daily practice.

FINAL THOUGHTS

So in the final analysis, we must understand that God is completely in control. He doesn't need help in being God. I'm still learning this today and every day. This book is just a chapter in my life that I want to disclose to you, the reader. It doesn't mean that I have arrived. It doesn't mean that I have made it. It only means that this is what I have accomplished thus far and there's more to come. As long as God has His hand in it, He will bring you further and deeper in Him than you've ever imagined. This book is just a stepping stone. I still have quite a long ways to go. I'm not there yet. As a matter of fact, I'm nowhere near it. But this is just an assignment that God has given me. I just wanted to share the few things that I learned thus far.

Your dreams, goals, visions, aspirations all have to have a starting place. You can't go anywhere in life if you don't have a starting point. The finish line may be far off, but this race is not given to the swift. This battle is not given to the strong. Just because you are wise doesn't mean that you'll have food to eat. You may be skillful at what you do, but it doesn't always lead to a life of riches and wealth. You may even be educated in a certain area, but it doesn't always lead to a successful life. But it is all decided by chance and opportunity. It's about being in the right place at the right time (Ecclesiastes 9-11). So you must be prepared when the opportunity comes. You have to at least be able to do all these things to position yourself for the opportunity.

Can you truly say to yourself that you will be prepared when the opportunity comes? Will you be ready? Are you at least doing the things necessary to position yourself for the opportunity or chance that may come? If you're not, then why are you wasting your time? That's what I believe this scripture is talking about. If you're not at least trying to position yourself with your skill, education, wisdom, strength, and your ability to execute these things, then what's the point of going through that process and not doing anything with it? There are certain things you have to do for opportunity to present itself. There will be times when you have to get up off your butts and go find the opportunity. Trust me! Opportunity won't fall in your laps. There has to be a sense of urgency.

Also, you must have a sense of direction. Direction can only come from God. If you don't have a sense of direction, then how will you know where to go or what to do? Paul says he doesn't run uncertainly or without definite aim. He goes on to say that he doesn't box like one beating the air or shadow box and striking without an adversary. However, like a boxer, he buffets his body, handles it roughly, disciplines his body by hardships, and subdues it. He says he does all this to be prepared to proclaim the Gospel to others and the things pertaining to it. He says he fears that if he doesn't prepare himself that he may be unfit, not able to stand the test, be unapproved, and rejected as counterfeit (1 Corinthians 9:24-27). Wow! So you have to be certain about the direction in which God has you going. Don't let people move you into a direction that God has not orchestrated for you. It definitely takes the process a lot longer to manifest itself. Amen?

GFSoldier Quotes:

When a person means well, it doesn't mean that their methods are necessarily accurate. You can do things with the right intentions and still have the wrong method of doing it. The best intentions do not always bring about the best results.

Telling the truth and being truthful doesn't always coincide. If you're telling or verbalizing the truth and your intentions are bad, that's worse than any lie you can come up with. Telling the truth with a deceitful heart is worse than lying itself.

Be very careful of those who wrongfully use the truth to defend, justify, and excuse their hidden subtleties.

Many people spend years making alterations of themselves having never to step up and make an actual change.

If the truth is given harshly and not harmlessly, then the person who is giving the truth is guilty of mishandling it. Normally when truth is being mishandled, more than likely the person receiving it won't be able to handle it either.

The truth can sometimes be a like a raw uncooked twenty-ounce steak. It's inedible. If you shove it down someone's throat, it becomes indigestible (cooked or uncooked) and they will eventually regurgitate. However, when it is well cooked, fully seasoned, it becomes edible. When it is cut into smaller pieces and fed to someone it allots more time for the person to chew on it and it will eventually become more digestible.

Being right doesn't necessarily mean that you are right. Just because you are correct with your facts does not always mean the timing was right for you say it. Many times we can have the wrong intentions when we're trying to be right. So as a result you can be correct and still be wrong because you lack the wisdom to be able to exercise sound judgment in your decision to speak in an orderly or time-sufficient manner. Yes! Sometimes you can be right at the wrong time.

People who are obsessed with being right often times don't know or acknowledge that they're actually being that way. There's nothing more dangerous than a self-righteous, stubborn, self-indulgent fool who's right all the time and never wrong. It normally means that they're not open to anyone's opinion but their own.

For those of us who quote the Bible without having the proper knowledge of the scripture, please understand, "quoting" Bible verses is not the same as "studying" the Word. It only means that you have become sufficient in the memorization of the scriptures but very deficient in the exegesis of it.

Just because you are anointed, does not mean that you're in a right relationship with God. You must not confuse your anointing with your humanity. Your anointing does not dispel your humanity.

Please understand, the Spirit of God will flow in the gift because there are lives at stake, lost souls that need to be saved, and people who need to be inspired. However, just because the anointing of the Spirit flows through you doesn't mean that the Spirit God lives in you.

When it comes to serving in the will of God, you must become strong enough to be weak.

You cannot be so caught up in the ministry of God that you forget to minister to God. You cannot get so caught in the external intricacies of God that you miss or neglect the internal intimacy of God. Make sure not to get so caught up in practical outward adorning tendencies, that you missed the spiritual inward propensities.

God has to be first in all that you do in ministry. Many times we equate doing the ministry of God or doing God's work with doing God's will. Just because you're doing God's work, it doesn't necessarily mean you're doing His will.

Good Morning Family! I'm heavily convicted this morning, but I must ask these questions to the married folk. Which one are you? Are you a husband/wife? Or Are you just a spouse? Do you have a marriage? Or are you just married? I ask these questions because there appears to be many couples who are "married" but don't have a "marriage." Spouse is just a mere title; a simple signing of documents to solidify the legality of two people being married by state law. Husband/wife is a ministry; where two people enter into a relationship and covenant with God and each other to develop a marriage. Being "married" is instant. However having a "marriage" is an ongoing and ever-growing process. We hold the "title" of spouse but have not yet embraced the "ministry" of husband or wife. Many of us want the title but don't want the ministry/responsibility that comes along with the title. Some of us are obsessed with wanting to be married so that we simply forget about or don't want the marriage. So I humbly implore you: If you're

196

not willing to die to yourself and/or give up yourself for the sake of marriage, then it's best that you stay single in an effort to avoid divorce. In this case, it really is better to say no than it is to say yes. Choose which one you will be.

NOTE TO THE READER:

In obedience to God, this book comes to you in the spirit of brokenness and a heart of contrition, which are sacrifices that are most pleasing to God. *Trifling to Transformed* will give an account and admission of the mistakes I've made, my purposeful insufficiencies, my deliberate acts of sin/evil, my inconsistencies, my shortcomings, and my trials. This will also give an account of how I am continuing to overcome these issues in my daily walk.

Side note: Just because you've been delivered doesn't mean you have arrived! Having the heart of contrition, I will also confess, with the spirit of repentance, some of my current struggles as they relate to the flesh and how the gift of exhortation (speaking publically) is helping me to cope with them. This is how the gift continues to save my life, especially when it is used correctly. We often encounter emotions that are very difficult to comprehend. Some emotions we do comprehend, but we often times neglect them. As a result, we either repress or suppress our emotions, only to have them show up unmonitored, unchecked, and at the most inopportune times.

Through verbal and literary artistry, *Trifling to Transformed* is a deliberate attempt to reveal some of these hidden emotions, especially the emotions that lead us to entertain ungodly thoughts and do ungodly things, all the while being under the anointing. Having the heart of contrition and the spirit of brokenness, coupled with integrity, I believe, is the quintessential embodiment and concrete foundation in which ministry should go forth.

This particular component of contrition is an opportunity for the minister of the gift to be open, honest, and transparent, as David was when he wrote the 38th and 51st Psalms. I pray that this book will be received with a heart of openness, empathy, and acceptance, and an understanding that is void of resistance. I must warn you, the reader: if you are too saved, too sanctified, and too filled with the Holy Ghost, then this book is not for you. There will be no need for you to read this because you already have it together.

However, if you have struggled or are currently wrestling with some issues as they relate to ministry or in your personal walk, then this is the book for you! We often times testify about being delivered. We also testify about struggles we used to deal with. But we very seldom talk about current struggles. I want to make an all-out effort to expose the flesh that we often times, consciously or subconsciously, carry with us in ministry and in our daily walk.

It is also my endeavor to enforce a no holds barred attempt to expose the godly and ungodly aspects of ministry, particularly, but not limited to, the artistic expression. With some poetry included, this book will also attempt to provide a comprehensive, informative, and testimonial examination of how the gift saved my life from the inside out. This will include correction, reproach, exhortation and encouragement that I personally received from God. This book will also give an account of how I was able to translate the gift of what I do artistically into what I do academically and professionally.

I must also warn you that some parts of this book will be quite uncomfortable, and somewhat painful to read, especially if the topic discussed is something that you're currently wrestling with. Tearing down strongholds can sometimes be a very painful process. Some things you will agree with, some things you will completely disagree with. If so, let's have some dialogue about this and continue to sharpen each other as we grow in God.

However, the primary objective of this book is to encourage you. I pray God blesses you as you read.

Trifling: *someone who is one or all of the following: dishonest, shady, secretive, a player, "all talk," without following through, not worthy of trust--in general, a lack of ethics or general morality (i.e.: worthless; insignificant or of very little importance).*

THANK YOUS

I want to thank God for people who have inspired me in what I do and have helped me along the way. My early inspirations: My grandmother, Helen Bennett Johnson; my sister, Delisha Boyd; My Niece Kristen Boyd; Bishop Paul S. Morton, Sr. Pastor Debra B Morton; my big brother, Calvin CC Clark and family, who taught me the true meaning of humility and servanthood. Christa Gayden, also known as Mother Wisdom, Jackie Hill Perry, Leonard Oracle Woodard, Terrence "Gifted the Flamethrowa" Veal, Dr. Frederick Douglas Haynes III, Pastor Efrem Windom, Pastor Derek L Winkley, Je'Mahl Ray, Tiffany Thompson and family, Passion for Christ Movement (P4CM), Jarrod Joseph and family Pervis Hall, Poet Se7en, Pastor Juan Rivera, J Errol Lewis, Spoken Life Chicago, TBAAL, Michael Guinn, Alexandria Gurley, Phea Shelton Kennedy, Lisa Selah Watkins, Shelton "Shakespeare" Alexander, Sunni Patterson, Reginald Boyd, Bishop Noel Jones, Dr. Michael Eric Dyson, and last but certainly not least, the Young Family: Monica Young (wife), Hilton C. Young, Jr., (son) and Lalaune Talford (daughter).

www.ingramcontent.com/pod-product-compliance
Lightning Source LLC
Chambersburg PA
CBHW051148120626
46547CB00012B/986